POLO IN INDIA

POLO IN INDIA

CAPTAIN G. J. YOUNGHUSBAND

Published by

Gyan Publishing House
5, Ansari Road
Daryaganj, New Delhi-110002
Phone: 011-47034999, 9811692060
E-mail: books@gyanbooks.com

Distribution Network
gyanbooks.com
India, USA, Canada, UK, Australia

ISBN: 978-93-6780-559-6 (HB)

First Published, 1890

2nd Impression 2024

Printed at: Gyan Press, Delhi.

POLO IN INDIA
Author: CAPTAIN G. J. YOUNGHUSBAND

POLO IN INDIA.

POLO IN INDIA.

BY

CAPTAIN G. J. YOUNGHUSBAND,

QUEEN'S OWN CORPS OF GUIDES.

W. H. ALLEN & CO.,

LONDON: 13 WATERLOO PLACE, PALL MALL. S.W.

AND CALCUTTA.

1890.

PREFACE.

It is with considerable diffidence that I venture to place before the polo-playing public this small book on the Game of Polo as played in India. I can hardly say that it "supplies a long-felt want," because I am afraid that the want of a really good book on Polo will still be felt after my humble effort is published. My only hope is that someone, more competent to write on the subject than I am, will, on seeing this book, rise in his wrath and forthwith give to the world a standard book on Polo worthy of his theme. If, meanwhile, any hints that may be found within are of any use in helping young and aspiring Polo teams on their road towards winning a Polo Tournament, my labours will not have been altogether in vain. My best thanks are due to the many kind people and distinguished players who have helped me in this work.

G. J. Y.

Junior Army and Navy Club,
January 1890.

CONTENTS.

CHAPTER V.

On Polo Sticks.

CHAPTER VI.

Regimental Polo Clubs.

CHAPTER VII.

En Route to a Tournament.

CHAPTER VIII.

Polo Tournaments.

CHAPTER IX.

Duties of Different Members of a Team.

CHAPTER X.

POLO IN INDIA.

CHAPTER I.

THE GAME OF POLO.

THE game of polo was originally adopted, we believe, from the Manipuris; and though in its present phase it is as unlike the original Manipuri game as anything well can be, yet the main features still remain—a man on a pony, hitting a ball with a stick, and striving to attain a certain object. We hardly dare say who actually introduced polo into India—indeed we do not rightly know—for many claim the honour, and all on apparently undisputable grounds. The fact most probably is that the game cropped up at several places in India at much about the same time, hence the differences of opinion. The first polo club formed in India of which we can find any record was started by the late Colonel R.

Stewart, then Superintendent of Cachar, in the year 1862. This club was composed chiefly of Manipuris and Planters. By the kind permission of Major-General G. Stewart, C.B., late of the Guides, a copy of the original rules of this club are given later on. The following interesting note is also furnished by General Stewart :—

I visited my brother in September 1862, and saw the game played at Cachar, and returning with sticks and balls in October of that year to Barrackpore, where I was stationed, I formed a club there, where we practised for some months, when the game was taken up by some Calcutta men, who also got up a club there. The first match was played between the Barrackpore Club and the Calcutta Club, on the Calcutta Maidan early in 1863. The only members of the Barrackpore Club whose names I remember were, besides myself, Colonel Arthur Broome, Bengal Cavalry; the late Colonel J. Broome, 2nd Punjab Cavalry ; the Hon. R. Napier (the present Lord Napier) ; Colonel Apperly, late 15th Bengal Cavalry ; a veterinary surgeon of the name of Farrell, and a Captain King, since deceased. The Calcutta players were chiefly merchants, one of whom went by the name of "Bobbie Hills," a little fellow, I think a relation of the General Hills who was in Kabul with Roberts. On my way up to Peshawur in May 1863, I stayed a few days with my brothers at Cawnpore and Mian Mir, and at each of those places I started the game, having brought up sticks and balls for the purpose. Again, in Peshawur, during 1863-64, polo or "kangai," as it was then called, was played regularly after I had started it. . . . "Polo" is the Tibetan name of the game. I have played at Skardo with the Tibetans ; they use a different stick or club. The stick now used in India is the original "kangai" stick. Bamboo balls were always used. As many as seven played on a side, two generally keeping goal. The ponies were 12-2, and the game was by no means a fast one.

From that time forth the game of polo has flourished and increased in popularity with every succeeding year, and a debt of gratitude is certainly due to the Stewart family for having contributed so largely to the introduction and incubation of this magnificent game. In northern India there is scarcely a station, however small, which is without its polo ground; and many regiments, both British and native, have a sufficient number of good players amongst their officers to make up their own game, however isolated their position may be. In southern India, owing chiefly, we believe, to the dearness and scarcity of ponies, the game does not flourish quite so well; but still it is everywhere most popular, and wherever possible it is played with great vigour.

From its earliest days, up to the institution of tournaments (in 1876, we believe), polo as a game of skill gradually improved, and at the same time gradually changed its character. It is barely ten years ago since we used to play on small handy ponies, and make elaborate gallery strokes, while the other seven players stood around or tittuped about waiting for their turn. This game, of course, died before the galloping game, and is now entirely obsolete in most parts of the world.

With the kind permission of the Editor of the *Civil and Military Gazette*, we give below a slight sketch of the rise and fall of successive systems, by "An Elderly Gentleman." Though his article is written in a frivolous strain, none the less he makes some points, which may be recommended to the reader's attention. After a few preliminary remarks, "An Elderly Gentleman" enters upon his self-appointed task of criticising the game of Polo, past and present, in the following words:—

Now that the yearly epidemic of tournaments is over, let us sit down comfortably and criticise tournaments in general, and this year's (1888) in particular. I don't play polo myself, thank goodness, and that makes it all the easier to criticise others; for, as we all know, "lookers on see most of the game."

Thanks to my friend Jones, who lent me a high dog-cart to sit in, and with the aid of a few technical details furnished by a rickety-looking little subaltern, in a very tight coat and very high collar who sat by me, I feel quite competent to give most of the foremost players of the day a few hints that will, without doubt, be useful to them.

Tournaments (my informant is the rickety-looking little subaltern above mentioned, whose name I have forgotten, but whom, for the sake of brevity we will call "Prig," meaning no offence thereby) were started before the Afghan War of 1878, but did not develop into the stern, cut-and-thrust, gladiatorial combats they have since become, till after that great historic event.

I myself distinctly remember the game in those olden days. I even played myself once or twice, and was thought rather good by the other fellows. We did not have any foolishness, such as hustling, and riding off and galloping about like maniacs. Not at all; we took our pleasures calmly. We cantered about gently, and admired the scenery, and when a ball came near us, we tippled it along serenely, knowing well that no one would be so ungentlemanly as to hustle us or crook our sticks. I can well remember my horror and speechless indignation when one day, a young whipper-snapper on my own side actually took the ball on from under my very nose, whilst I was making a very majestic run, and had the complacency to hit the goal which I had intended to hit myself very shortly.

Such like actions were the death-knell of the old game. It soon became evident that a team hitting up from one to another could walk round a team who made individual runs on the old system.

The next development of the game, which was initiated about eight years ago, was the hustling, bustling, and general suppression of the enemy's "back" by a "flying man," usually a light-weight, mounted on very fast and handy ponies. This manœuvre, when it was first invented, was most paying; and many a match and tournament was virtually won or lost by the "flying man."

Since then, however, whether it is that the "flying man" does not stick to business as much as he used to do, or whether it is that the race of "backs" has learnt how to dodge him, neither I nor my friend Prig can say; but the fact remains that we have not this year seen a single "flying man" thoroughly collar the opposite "back" from start to finish.

The first result of this institution of a "flying man" was to instil a wholesome fear into the opposite "back," to cramp him, and to make him afraid to move up into the game; he stood afar off, and hit long hits up to the others, whenever by the kindness of fate and the "flying man" he was allowed to hit anything at all. Now, however, that diffidence has worn off, and we see the "back" quite ignoring the "flying man," and playing with great vigour and brilliancy. In fact, "back" and "No. 2" seem to be the playing men, both in attack and defence, and not, as formerly, "Nos. 2 and 3."

Having thus briefly traced the game in its various phases up to the present date, let us have a look at this year's tournaments.

To begin with the ponies. Prig tells me that at a solemn conclave held last year by a large gathering of polo players, it was unanimously decided to measure every pony this year before it was allowed to play in a tournament. This seemed very right and proper; and we looked forward with interest and considerable curiosity, in the hopes of learning how some of the larger horses played on last year would be induced to pass under the 13-3 standard. By the way, it is quite extraordinary how the vast majority of ponies have managed to grow an inch since last year. Perhaps it may have struck me more forcibly than most people, for I was on furlough at the time the polo height was raised from 13-2 to 13-3, and did not hear of it; so that on my return, I was surprised to find confidential old tatooes that I had known all my life as "easy 13-2" swaggering around and calling themselves "a good 13-3," without a blush. However, that is neither here nor there; none of us stick much at an inch now-a-days; but it really did rouse our keenest curiosity to find out how some fellows would manage to make quite large horses, animals that would would put many a troop horse to shame, measure 13-3. We were disappointed, however; their owners are still possessed of the dark and bloody mystery, which we hoped to see unravelled before our eyes.

In one tournament the ponies certainly were measured, and four of the largest excluded at first; but on a second view they evidently seemed to look smaller, and were finally passed and allowed to play.

In the other tournaments no attempt at measurement was made, and we saw nothing to prevent ponies of any size being ridden in them. That brings us to our first point, and that is, if the size of ponies is entirely ignored, in spite of the rule on the subject, what is the good of having a rule at all—why not leave the height question entirely to settle itself? If I were an orator, I should go down and make a speech on the subject at the next polo meeting; but I am not, and, therefore, any fellow who can talk may take the whole of this article, and grind it out to that solemn conclave, and swear it is all his own, without let or hindrance from me. As long as the size of the ground remains fixed, *i.e.* is 300 yards by 200 yards, I feel sure that the height question will settle itself. Players will find that a 15-hand waler, though he will outpace a pony in a straight run, will take such a long time turning and be running out so often, and be generally so cumbersome and unwieldy, that he will be voted out of place at once; and so with every size until we get down to about 14 hands, and that, between you and I and the bedpost, is really the height of most of this year's 13-3 ponies. Mind, my proposition is entirely on the condition that the ground is not enlarged; for, of course, on a ground measuring 1,500 yards by 750 yards, the big horses would have it all their own way. In those pre-historic times, when polo was first beginning, grounds were any size, according to the taste and fancy of the maker. Ours was 150 yards by 100 yards; and though there was no very strict rule about ponies, we found that a pony measuring from 12-2 to 13 hands was the best animal for a ground of this size.

On this subject, therefore, Prig and I are agreed—either ponies should be measured by a committee of independent persons, or else the entire rule about height should be abolished, and the matter left to settle itself. We hope that before next year the present unsatisfactory state of affairs will be altered.

Well, we have seen the ponies marched past, and have joined in the free and elegant chaff which greets any particularly full-grown leviathan as he is led round. I ask Prig what the price of that rather nice looking pony would be. I have a mind to buy a hack for my wife to ride in the hills.

"Six hundred rupees," says he, gently chewing a toothpick.

"Ghosts of my fathers!—Six hundred rupees for a polo pony. Impossible!"

"Impossible? Why that next one is advertised for eight hundred." And to think that in my days a first-class pony went begging at Rs. 60, and only very high fellows like colonels of cavalry regiments and commissioners ever ran to such high prices as Rs. 100. Here is a subject for a sermon diluted with tears.

"Who profits by this enormous rise?"

"No one much, except the dealers," says Prig.

I think he is right. He went on to tell me that no one thinks much of a pony now-a-days, unless he is high priced; a hint which I promptly acted upon by selling a three-cornered beast I have had on my hands for some time for Rs. 350. He had previously been on the market for months, at an upset price of Rs. 150, without raising an offer. I myself am pretty well off, and can afford a six-hundred-rupee pony at a pinch; but I am lost in a perfect whirlwind of conjecture as to whence Prig and his fellow subalterns who, to my certain knowledge, have not any private means at all, manage to get the wherewithal to buy not only one, but four or five of these very costly ponies. I am rather afraid of Prig, though he is so young; but some day I mean to pluck up courage and ask him. There were regimental teams of ponies on the ground valued at Rs. 10,000.

Outsiders and women immediately exclaim, "How very shocking! What a sinful waste of money. What adequate return do you get for this outlay?" My dear old ladies, of both sexes, believe me that the indirect return in kind, not money, is beyond all computation. Polo has, in conjunction with pig-sticking, done more towards teaching our young cavalry officers that dash, nerve, steadiness, seat and discipline, which are the boast and pride of the English nation, than any other pastimes or sports. Next time you are in Europe, just saunter round and look at a French, or German, or Russian officer. I assure you he is a perfect tailor on horseback compared to the average British youngster.

This brings us to our second proposition, and that is, that Government, taking into consideration the great advantage accruing indirectly to its mounted services from the playing of the game of polo, shall do something to lighten the burden of expense borne by the officers, such as the granting of free passes to and from tournaments, and even the loan of money, without charging interest, to polo clubs, and so on.

I know "Government," whoever it is, will jeer at this; it always does cast the cold and fishy eye of disdain on any proposition which entails the spending of the smallest coin of the realm. My omniscient and precocious friend, Prig, says that "Government" is a Babu,* which perhaps accounts for it.

However, whilst we have been wandering off into these abstruse subjects, the game has begun, and we settle ourselves down to watch and criticise it. As before mentioned, the point that strikes us first and most forcibly is the immense improvement in the *rôle* of the "back" since we last saw a tournament. Out of nearly a score of teams we have seen this year, the "back" has been, almost invariably, the most brilliant and dashing player. Formerly the heaviest man in a team was put "back," as a matter of course, a good solid heavy charging body, like the bull-dog in a bobbery pack. Now the "back" is a light weight, mounted on the speediest of ponies, and is to be seen here, there, and everywhere. "No. 3" seems to have the most uninteresting time of them all, for he has to be in readiness to drop back when the "back" makes a run, and to keep him from being hustled during a retreat. "No. 2" is, as formerly, the playing man of the team. "No. 1," the "flying man," disappointed us this year; he seemed either to have lost heart and to be sick of pursuing the "back," or else—and this is an unpardonable offence—he was playing for the gallery, bitten, like many youngsters, with a mania for seeing his name in the newspapers as having hit a goal or made a run. Of course we do not refer to the "flying man," who having a much faster pony than the opposing "back," walked clean away from him and hit goals; but to those, and there were many of them, who, instead of riding honestly and hard for "No. 2," were constantly trying to make unprofitable strokes on their own little hooks.

In polo, as in war, it is the veteran, the old soldier, the old polo player, who comes to the front in a tight corner. I don't mean very

* A native clerk, often a product of lower Bengal, whose pen is his sword, and frothy nothings his shield and buckler.

old—not as old as I am—but a man who has been through three or four tournaments before. There is Jones, for instance; I know half-a-dozen youngsters who can play twice as well as he can in an ordinary station game, but in a tournament he walks round them. He plays about the same, perhaps better than usual; and they, from one cause or another, play very much under their usual form. A team of veterans is two goals better than a team of young soldiers, all other things being equal. Pondering over past years, it strikes us that an undue advantage is given to that regiment which plays on its own ground. Taking Umballa, for instance, what a very large proportion of Umballa regiments have won the various cups when the tournament has been held there! One year, if not two, all the three cups went to Umballa regiments. We don't wish to be ungracious, or dim the splendours of old victories, but we should have been very sorry to have backed the victors to repeat their victory on neutral ground. This year, another instance turned up, briefly, as follows:—A regiment, which was considered completely out of the betting, whose form was known, and had been thoroughly gauged in out-station matches, suddenly came to the front, the tournament being held on its own ground, and as nearly as possible walked that tournament.

Our third proposition, then, is: That the regiment playing on its own ground shall be handicapped either one or two goals, as may be hereafter decided.

* * * * *

I do hope that polo will not degenerate into pot-hunting. Honour and glory and a challenge cup is quite enough for the true sportsman. It seems a pity that all did not follow the example of the infantry, in making their cup a permanent challenge cup never to be won.* An outward and visible sign of our victory is a pleasant and soothing sight on a mess-table, as long as we remain victors; but I, for one, don't feel the least pride in, or affection for, a cup won years before my time by a by-gone generation.

In fact, to sum up, the points to which "An Elderly

* All the polo cups are now, I believe, permanent challenge cups.—G. J. Y.

Gentleman" wishes to draw particular attention are :—

(1) The measurement (or rather non-measurement) of ponies.

(2) Aid and encouragement of the game by those in power.

(3) The handicapping of the regiment which plays on its own ground in a tournament.

As regards (1) the measurement of ponies, we are at complete accord with him. If the rule is that no pony shall be over 13-3 in height with shoes, let us by all means stick by our rule and have every single pony measured by an independent committee on the ground the day before the tournament. If, on the other hand, there is no particular object in making the height a fixed height, then by all means let us abolish a vexatious and unobserved rule; and, as our critic suggests, "allow the height question to settle itself." In England the height is supposed to be fourteen hands, but no one is particular to an inch or two; and we have before now seen a 15-hand horse playing in an ordinary game at Aldershot. In tournaments at home, as in India, any very outrageous infringement of the height rule would probably raise an objection; but an inch more or less passes in the crowd unnoticed.

The whole secret of this seeming slackness lies in a nutshell. As the rule at present stands, all the ponies belonging to the competing teams are ordered to parade at a certain place at a certain hour for inspection and approval. They are there and then led past in single file, and the captain of any team is empowered to stop and have measured on the spot any of his opponent's ponies, concerning whose qualifications as to height he has any doubt. Then, why doesn't he exercise his right? There are two reasons; the first is that it is not customary and would be considered perhaps impolite to cast doubt on the good faith of an opponent; and, secondly, we are inclined to think, chiefly because he is hardly prepared on the spur of the moment to subject his own team of ponies to the severe counter-measurement which would be immediately demanded by his opponents, *there and then.* The fact is that many ponies, when taken quietly, as they stand eating their food in their stables, for instance, will exactly measure the required height. Some of these ponies will measure the same anywhere under any circumstances, whilst others directly they get outside, perhaps a little excited amongst other ponies, or what not, will measure a good inch higher than they did in a state of quiescence. No captain, therefore, cares to run the risk of finding that perhaps some of his best ponies will not measure, and are therefore disqualified from playing at the last moment, when it is impossible to replace them; he therefore avoids criticism on his own ponies by viewing with a lenient eye his opponent's ponies. There is more at stake than the casual observer imagines in the failure to measure of a pony at a tournament; for putting aside the possibly irremediable loss in playing power to the team that the pony belongs to, there is the actual heavy pecuniary loss to the owner of the disqualified pony. The pony before being disqualified may be worth Rs. 1,000; but the moment he is disqualified from playing in a tournament his value falls with one fell sweep to that of a lady's hack or trapper, perhaps from Rs. 1,000 to Rs. 300. The odd seven hundred rupees being his polo-playing value. This may be taken as an exaggerated case of the matter under discussion, but by no means an impossible one.

One thing seems clear, as our critic definitely puts it, and that is that the present unsatisfactory state of affairs should have the serious attention of polo players. It may not be inappropriate to point out here the anomaly of the only system of horse measurement now in vogue, and that is that the height of a horse is alone fixed by his height in hands and inches from the level ground to the top of his withers. The object of measurement is, we imagine, to bring horses or ponies of the same powers as to size and speed into as fair and even a category as possible. Does measurement to the top of a horse's withers do so? We think not. All the galloping power of a horse is behind; and though the height or lowness of a horse's withers may make a very appreciable difference in the comfort of his paces as a hack, and in his handiness, yet our individual experience has failed to show us that it makes an appreciable difference in his galloping power—in his pace, that is to say—which is the point at issue. To measure horses to the top of the quarters instead of to the top of the withers would, we are inclined to think, be a surer guarantee of bringing animals of the same galloping powers together than the present system of measurement. It may be an incorrect supposition, but it appears to us that a system which was originally invented in England for the measurement of hacks, chargers, and harness horses, in which classes height at the withers is a consideration, has been applied without much relevance to racing and polo ponies, where height at the withers has, we take it, little to do with the powers it is intended to gauge.

Secondly "An Elderly Gentleman" asks for more encouragement and assistance from the powers that be, on the plea that polo improves, to an appreciable degree the horsemanship and equestrian skill of young officers, and especially of young cavalry and staff officers, whose riding is part and parcel of their profession. Perhaps we can hardly expect a Government whose every spare rupee is required for Imperial defence works and strategic railways to give pecuniary aid; but certainly in the matter of railing teams free of cost to and from tournaments on all Government lines, a great and very appreciable boon would be granted, which would cost the donor nothing more than would result in the infinitesimal deterioration to the rolling stock, employed once a year only be it remembered, in carrying teams of ponies to and from the *rendezvous*.

The third point which our friendly polo critic wishes to be brought to notice is what he calls the undue advantage which appears to accrue to that team which happens to be stationed at the place where the tournament is held, and which consequently plays on its own ground, or on a ground it is well accustomed to, against teams whose members and ponies are playing on a foreign ground, where the conditions of soil, light, &c. are different to those they are accustomed to. In support, he mentions the fact that for several years, when the different tournaments were played at Umballa, the local regiments carried off all the cups. That there is a good deal of reason in this argument most of us, from our own experience, will be able to affirm ; to suggest a remedy is a much more difficult problem.

A case in point comes to our recollection at this moment. Our own regimental team was playing an out-station match with another regiment on the latter's ground: we were defeated by four goals to three. Shortly afterwards a return match was played on our ground, and we defeated the former victors by eight goals to one. Making every allowance for questions of whether one team or the other was in

" good form " or " bad form " on particular dates, we are bound, in this case, to allow that the all-important factor was the ground played on. There are only two remedies which occur to us beside the one suggested (handicapping the home regiment), and they are :—(1) To pitch a camp and clear a ground in some entirely neutral country, and play out the tournament there; or (2) oblige the victorious team, if winning on its own ground, to clench the victory by defeating its opponents again on the latter's own ground. The former of these two alternatives appears the most feasible; for there is plenty of waste land in many parts of India which could in a few months be turned into a first-class polo ground, kept up at little or no expense. The second alternative would perhaps tend to drag out a tournament unduly, and a tie might be the result after all. Perhaps, in lieu of *obliging* the home team to play again, it would be better to word the suggestion " the home team, if victorious, is liable to be challenged to a return match on another ground." However, we are only, for our part, attempting to open the door to discussion, and hope that abler pens and more experienced polo-players will endeavour to erase these blots on the game, if blots they may be considered.

CHAPTER II.

THE RULES OF POLO.

THE first club rules of which we can find any reliable record are those of the Cachar Club. They are given below *in toto,* as likely some day to prove of historic interest. Further on in this chapter will be found the rules of polo, as revised at the Polo Meeting at Umballa in 1887.

Rules of the game of "Kangjai,"* as determined at a meeting of the Cachar Kangjai Club held at Silchar, 1st January 1863 :—

I.—The limits of the ground should be marked off with a small ditch a few inches in depth, as in sketch.

II.—The ball should be placed at C, and one of each side endeavour simultaneously to strike it.

III.—When the ball is struck off the ground, either across the line A B or D E, as shown by the dotted line *a b*, umpires, or a bystander, should throw it on again in a direction perpendicular to A B, as marked by the dotted line *b c*.

IV.—When the ball is struck off the ground, either across the line A B or D E, as shown by the dotted line *d e*, and is beyond the

* The Manipuri name for polo.

goal, it is to be brought back to the point *f*, and thrown on the ground perpendicular to the side line.

V.—When the ball is struck over at any of the corners ta shown by the dotted line *i*, it is to be brought to the corner, and struck thence towards *c* by one of the side whose goal was so nearly invaded, as shown in the line *i* D *g*.

VI.—No player is willingly to strike either his antagonist or his antagonist's horse.

VII.—No player is to lay his hand on his antagonist or his antagonist's rein.

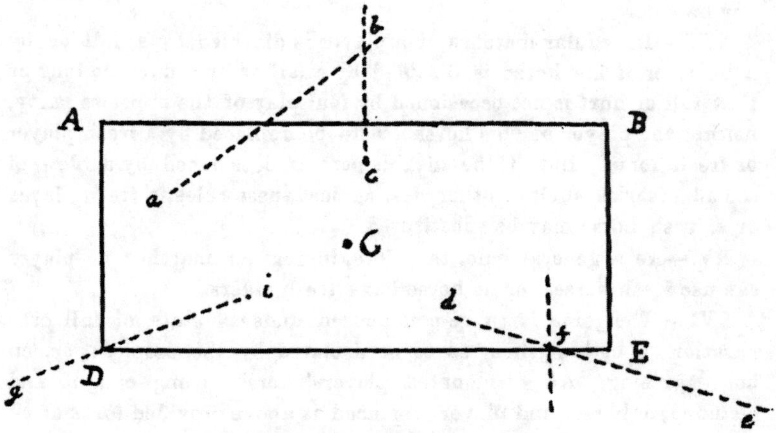

A B should be 200 yards long, and A D 120 yards.

VIII.—Any player, when his antagonist is about to strike the ball, may strike at his antagonist's stick or hook it, but only when the ball is about to be struck or in the neighbourhood of the ball when there is a rush.

IX.—Any player may interpose his horse before his antagonist's so as to prevent his antagonist from reaching the ball, whether in full career or at the slow pace; and this despite the immediate neighbourhood of the ball.

X.—When a stick is broken, its owner is to ride out of the ground to replace it, and on no account is anyone to run in with a stick to him.

XI.—When a stick is dropped, the rider is to dismount and pick it up himself, or one of his side may do it for him, but no outsider is to run in to do so.

XII.—When any derangement occurs in a player's horse-gear, he is likewise to ride out and have it repaired, unless he chooses to play on with it as it is, but on no account is anyone to come on to the ground to repair it.

XIII.—When any player is dismounted he is likewise to catch his own horse, to mount again, or one of his own side may catch it for him; as long as the horse runs off the ground, it may be caught by any outsider.

XIV.—In regular matches, if a player is disabled by a fall or by a hurt, or if his horse is disabled by a fall or by a hurt, so long as that fall or hurt is not occasioned by foul play of the opposite party, neither the player nor his horse are to be replaced by a fresh player or fresh horse. But if the disablement is occasioned by a blow of the adversaries' stick or otherwise, against these rules, a fresh player or a fresh horse may be substituted.

XV.—As a general rule, therefore, in regular matches no player can use fresh horses, or no horse have fresh riders.

XVI.—The game is to be commenced under a state of full preparation of both parties, so to be declared by the umpire; or, on both agreeing. All dismounted players' horses being caught and mounted, or horses and players replaced as above provided for, but no dismounting or disablement is to interfere with the course of the game when once begun.

XVII.—When the ball goes off the ground it is not immediately to be flung on again at the feet of any particular player's horse, but, after a time, on to the middle of the ground, when a sufficient number of both sides are there to receive it.

XVIII.—When a player catches the ball in his hands, he can strike it towards his adversaries' goal by tossing it up and hitting it with his stick, and to give him room to do this, he can ride away to clear himself of his enemies; but he can carry the ball no nearer to his adversaries' goal than the place where he first caught it.

XIX.—No dismounted player can strike the ball while he is on foot.

XX.—Spurs and whips may be freely used, but only on the rider's own horse; to beat an adversary's horse is foul play.

XXI.—No man on foot (save dismounted riders), or dogs, or cattle, to be allowed on the ground.

XXII.—It is to be understood that no player shall be under the influence of Bhang-gouja or spirituous liquors.

XXIII.—Any direct or wilful act of foul play, when it shall have been so declared by the umpire or umpires, shall at once be declared to have lost the game in a regular match.

It will be seen from a comparison of the above rules with those now in vogue, which are given later on, that the main elements of the game were much the same then as they are now. Rule IX. could not, of course, stand in the present galloping game without giving an undue amount of business to the undertaker. Rule XV. infers that it was usual for a player to use only one pony during a game; a task physically impossible for any pony in the present game. Rule XX. enacts that a rider shall use neither whip nor spurs (!) on his *neighbour's* pony. We should like to see a rule introduced in India forbidding the use of anything but dummy spurs in a tournament or match. Few men know how to use spurs, and fewer still are cool enough to use them with profit, either to themselves or their mounts, in the excitement of a tournament. Rule XXII. is a quaint old rule, for which there is no necessity in these days, in which, according to Mr. Corney Grain, a new-pattern subaltern drinks nothing but lemon-squashes, and those weak.

Rules as revised at Umballa, March 1887 :—

1. A committee, to be composed of three gentlemen not playing in the tournament, shall be chosen by the Honorary Secretary at the meeting—subject to the approval of the competitors—whose decision shall be final in all matters.

The committee shall measure the ponies; two of them shall act as umpires, or nominate others to act as such.

2. Each team shall be composed of four officers, who shall not be changed during the meeting—unless through any accident, sickness or unavoidable absence, any of them are not able to play, when the committee shall have the power of allowing the team to be made up by other officers of the same regiment.

3. To start the game, the umpire shall have the ball placed in the centre of the ground. Two players on opposite sides shall cross their sticks, heads upwards, over the ball, after which any player may strike the ball.

4. The ball shall be of bamboo root, about 10½ inches in circumference, and 4 ozs. in weight.

5. The ground shall be as nearly as possible 300 yards long by 200 yards wide, and shall be defined by a thinly cut line.

6. The goal flags shall be 22 feet apart.

7. Ponies to measure 13-3 without any allowance for shoes. Racing certificates not accepted. Every pony to be measured by the committee before being played, and no pony to be entered in the book unless he has actually played in that year's tournament.

8. Each game shall consist of 6 periods of 8 minutes each, exclusive of stoppages. Time shall not be called while the ball is in play, unless the game shall have lasted 48 minutes, when time shall be called irrespective of the ball being in play. (This applies only to the Inter-Regimental Tournament; at the other tournaments, either four or five periods only are played.)

In the event of a tie, the game shall be continued for another eight minutes, the goal flags being placed 44 feet apart. If still a tie, the game shall be continued until one side gets a goal. No team shall be compelled to play on two consecutive days.

9. Three minutes interval shall be allowed after every ten minutes' actual play, and after every goal; it being optional if both sides agree to have no interval. Time may be called whenever the ball is

out of play, and the game stopped for two minutes, at the expiration of which time the umpires shall call play.

10. It is a goal if the ball is hit between the posts, or over the posts if in the opinion of the umpire it would have gone between the posts produced.

11. Sides shall be changed after every goal. Should the game continue thirty minutes without a goal being obtained, sides shall be changed after thirty minutes' actual play, but should any goal afterwards be obtained, sides shall be changed for that goal, and for any subsequent goal, without reference to time.

12. The ball must go over and clear of the line to be out, and over and clear of the line to count a goal.

The ball on being hit out at the side line shall be thrown in underhand by one of the umpires, or by anyone deputed by them to do so, in a straight line at right angles to the line, and as hard as possible —the ball to touch the ground before passing the side line. The thrower-in to be on foot.

13. No player shall cross or ride dangerously.

If two players are riding to hit the ball from different directions, and a collision appears probable, the player in possession of the ball, *i.e.* he who hit the ball last, or has come in the direction from which the ball was last hit, must be given way to.

14. No player shall hit the ball, or in any way prevent the opposite side from hitting the ball when he is off-side. No player having been off-side shall take any part in the game unless the ball has been struck since he has become on-side.

15. A player is off-side, when at the time of the ball being hit he has no one of the opposite side between him and the adversary's goal line, and he is neither in possession of the ball nor backing up one of his own side. The position of the players should be considered at the time the ball is last hit, *i.e.* a player if on-side when the ball is last hit remains on-side till it is hit again.

16. No player shall put his stick over his adversary's pony, either in front or behind, nor put his stick in front of a pony's legs, so as to endanger tripping the pony up; nor shall any player in any way impede the stick of any other player who is not actually on the ball.

That no player shall crook his adversary's stick unless he is on the same side of the pony as the ball, or immediately behind.

17. No player shall throw. hit with his open hand, or carry the

ball. Should the ball lodge anywhere about his person, or about his pony, he shall dislodge it as soon as possible.

18. If, in the opinion of the umpire, the ball is sufficiently damaged to interfere with the game, he shall stop the game, and a new ball shall be thrown in from the side line nearest to where the ball was broken, and at right angles to it.

19. The umpires shall have the power of ordering off the ground any player who, after having been warned, plays unfairly or rides dangerously. Such player not to be replaced by anyone belonging to his regiment.

20. The umpires shall have the power of ordering off the ground any pony they may consider dangerous.

21. No goals shall be counted which have been obtained by unfair play. Any infringement of the rules constitutes unfair play, or a foul.

22. In case of a foul being declared, the umpire shall stop the game, and either of the two following penalties may be claimed by the side which has been declared to have been fouled.

1st. A free hit from where the ball was when the foul occurred, and none of the opposite side to be within ten yards of the ball. But if the foul occurs near the goal of the side which causes the foul, a free hit shall be given from a spot not within 13 yards of the goal, but as near as possible to where the foul occurred.

2nd. That the side which caused the foul take the ball back, and hit it off from behind their own goal line.

23. If the ball is hit behind the back line by one of the opposite side, it shall be hit off by one of the side whose line it is from a spot as near as possible to that at which it crossed the line. None of the opposite side shall stand within 30 yards of the back line until the ball is hit off. If the ball is hit behind the back line by one of the side whose line it is, it shall be hit off from the nearest corner by one of the opposite side, but no other player of that side shall stand within 30 yards of the back line until the ball is hit off. The other side shall stand behind their own goal line. The ball shall be considered to have been hit off when it has been brought more than three yards from the back line.

Small flags shall be placed on the side lines to mark 3 and 30 yards from the back line.

24. The time for beginning play shall be fixed, so that the hour's play, together with the time for stoppages, be completed before dusk.

25. The umpires shall have the power of ordering play to begin, notwithstanding the absence of any player after the time fixed.

26. Ponies shall be *bonâ fide* and unconditionally the property of the officers, non-commissioned officers, or men of the regiment or batteries which the team represents.

Captains of teams to certify to this fact before play begins.

27. No person, other than the umpires and players, shall come on the ground while the ball is in play

28. In riding off or hustling, no player shall make use of his arm below the elbow.

29. No pony shall play for two different regiments during one tournament.

In comparing the old game with its modern development, the main elements which will be noticed are: (1) the increase of pace; (2) the increase of the size of the ponies, and of the size of the ground; and (3) the subordination of individual play to the combined operations of a team. The old game died before the new game directly it came to a question of which was the most effective in a tournament. And though we are quite ready to acknowledge that the present system is the most paying, in fact, the only paying one in a closely-contested match, yet we cannot help thinking that polo has lost many of its former charms as a game of skill. Formerly every man in a team was a skilled player, using his stick with the freedom and ease of a racquet-bat: his pony was small, and his stick long, and he could take his time over every stroke. We will not say it was unheard of to hustle a man, and the crooking of sticks was sometimes resorted to, but only as a last resource to save a goal, or at some such critical moment. There was a sort of unwritten law that though hustling and bustling were permissible, yet it was not the correct thing to habitually employ them as part of the game. When we come to look back, there certainly was a considerable amount of common sense and justice in the old view; for we have only to apply hustling and the crooking of sticks to any other game to be at once struck with its absurdity. Suppose, for instance, at cricket, the wicket-keeper were allowed to hustle the batsman—to push him over, we will say, just as he is going to hit the ball; or, suppose that, in a four game of racquets, one of the partners on each side was told off throughout the game to crook the adversaries' racquets, or to hem one of them in the corner of the court, and prevent his hitting the ball at all, it is manifest that the character of that game would be quite altered, and, according to present lights, entirely spoilt. In the same way, and for the same reason, the old and original game of polo appears spoilt to one of the old class of players. We certainly sympathize with him a good deal, and should be glad to see, at any rate, a partial return to the old game. At present, out of a team of four men, one is told off to confine himself entirely to the suppression of the enemy's "back"; and another is told off to look after and annoy the enemy's "No. 2"; so that it comes to this, that every member of a team is either engaged in annoying someone else, or being annoyed himself, in hustling or in being hustled. It would not be fair to point out an evil, if evil it is considered, without suggesting a remedy for it. Our remedy is so sweeping that we are afraid most people will stand aghast at its radical nature. It is, in fact, to abolish hustling altogether. Of course, such a measure would entirely alter the present nature of the game, and it would take some little time to get accustomed to the change, but we feel sure that the change would be for the better, besides eliminating one of the great dangers of the game, one which is the cause directly or indirectly of many of the fatal accidents that occur.

At Clifton a dozen or more years ago "hacking over" at football was abolished, and we all decided that Rugby football was a doomed game in consequence; that it would never be the same thing again, and that we might as well ask our sisters and cousins to join in the new and as we thought ladylike game. But we were quite mistaken, the rule altered the game very materially, and eliminated an element of roughness, it is true, but no one, the game included, was any the worse for the change. In the same way, though no doubt the abolition of hustling at polo would be strongly opposed at first, and more especially so by those who have been born and bred to the present game, yet we cannot help thinking that in the long run the game will be benefited by some such alteration of the present rules. Indirectly, we would also prophesy a great saving to the pockets of polo players in general, for there is no doubt about it that a larger number of ponies is required nowadays, and each pony owing to the severe strain has a shorter career than in former days; both of which facts result in making polo the severe drain it often is on a player's resources. It will be objected that hustling being abolished everyone, all round, would be hitting goals by the score. If on trial this were found to be the case, it might easily be remedied by placing the goal posts closer together; so close, in fact, that it would require a really skilful stroke to hit a goal.

It will strike players of Rugby football as a curious anomaly that nothing but clean hit goals count towards victory in polo, whereas a "hit behind," though it may miss the goal only by an inch, and is to all intents and purposes as good a stroke as the more fortunate one, counts nothing towards a win. To remove this anomaly we should be glad to see a rule introduced which, as in Rugby football, would ascribe a certain number of marks towards a win for every "hit behind" that passed within say twenty, or ten, yards of the goal post on either side. We have seen victory go the wrong team so often from this cause that it seems only right to legislate on the subject. One occasion is particularly engraved on our memory, on which one team having penned their opponents from start to finish, had had shot after shot at the enemy's goal, only missing it again and again by a hair's breadth. At the call of time, as neither team had scored a goal, it was decided, in accordance with the rules laid down on the subject, that the goals should be widened to double the usual width and play continued till one side or the other scored a win. Almost immediately, by a lucky fluke, the team which had proved immeasureably inferior throughout the match scored a goal and won the tie. If "hits behind" had counted the verdict would have gone to the other and, as everyone could see, the better team. Most polo players will be able from their own experience to corroborate the contention that a certain anomaly does exist in this connection.

CHAPTER III.

ON POLO PONIES.

Where money is no object the problem of mounting a polo team is very much simplified; and it is advisable under these circumstances to buy the best "trained" ponies that are to be obtained. The most favourable time to do so would be after the polo tournaments, in March of each year. The purchaser can watch the tournaments all through, and, fixing on the best ponies, buy them regardless of cost, for it will as a rule be found that, though not advertised for sale, nearly every pony has his price, although it may be almost a prohibitive one. Soundness, age, size, appearance, sink into the background as almost secondary considerations when thus purchasing, for as long as the pony is very fast, handy, and true, and can play perfectly for five minutes during a tournament, we have got all we want. That is where the long purse comes in; a poor man cannot or certainly ought not, to be able to afford to buy a "screw," whereas a rich man can. In cases where money is a matter of considerable importance, and the regimental team aims at being mounted well at a moderate cost, the problem is much more complicated. There are two classes of pony in the market: one is the raw pony, bought either from a horse-dealer or the native breeder in the horse-breeding districts; and the other is the "trained" polo pony, which has been bought and trained by other hands, and which is usually purchased from a European. In price, if the buyer buys with discrimination, there should be a good deal of difference between the prices of the former and the latter. But before trusting to one's own unaided judgment in purchasing, in either case, it is most necessary to have a fairly clear understanding regarding a few preliminary matters. It is, in the first place, necessary to be an accurate judge of soundness and unsoundness, and the aging of a horse. Next, a certain amount of experience in purchasing is required; and most men have had to pay pretty heavily to gain this experience; further, a knowledge of the best points to be looked for in a pony, and also of the general shape and look of a model polo pony, are required. Judges of horse-flesh are, I might almost say, born; though even a born judge requires practice and experience. There are men who, if they live to be a hundred, will never know a good horse from a bad one; whilst others, even in the whirl and confusion of an Indian fair, will "spot" the likely ones with almost unerring accuracy. The latter are what may be called born judges; for both they and their less fortunate brethren who have a happy knack of *always* buying the wrong horses and ponies may have had exactly the same practice and experience, and yet one knows a good horse when he sees it and the other does not. This former class of judge is, I am afraid, in danger of becoming a relic of the past, in these days of remount committees. Formerly each regiment bought for itself, through one of its officers: these officers, being in a state of competition with one another, had to exercise their faculties for distinguishing a good horse from a bad one almost at a glance; and the man who could do so best, mounted his regiment on the best horses. Further, the purchaser could year by year watch the working of his purchases, seeing where his errors in judgment came in, and learning to avoid them in future. For the only way to become a first-class judge is to have experience on a very large scale, our judgment being tempered and corrected by having our failures and successes, working side by side, constantly before our eyes. In pony buying alone it is difficult for anyone, except a horse-dealer, to get experience on this same large scale; and it is therefore all the more important that the would-be purchaser should be fairly well up in the veterinary part of a judge's education before attempting to buy.

Taking, first, the raw pony. There are raw ponies, and raw ponies: there is the pony which, coming straight from the fields, will go into a game of polo and play "like a book" without any training whatever; and there is, on the other hand, and this is the pony most frequently met with, the animal which requires very careful training and handling before it is fit to take its place in the game. The former class will generally be found to consist of coarse-bred stallions or geldings which have led a virtuous and sober life, their sole occupation having been to transport fat bunniahs or zemindars sedately and securely from village to village. The latter class will consist generally of highly mettled, well-bred mares or stallions which have been bred for the market, and allowed to run wild all their lives, and which have been seldom or ever ridden in the days of their youth. Now there is not one man in fifty who can train one of this latter class successfully, whereas the most inexperienced of youngsters can train one of the former. These two very facts open the door to many failures. A young fellow, either by luck or aided by a friend's judgment, buys one of the former class, and finds after a few weeks' education that it plays beautifully; he thereupon, certainly with some excuse, concludes that he is a heaven-born horsebreaker, and determines to make his fortune without further delay by buying raw ponies for a song, and selling them for vast sums when trained to polo. And it is only when he comes across a highly-mettled animal, as described in our second category, that he sees how much he himself has to learn before he is competent to teach his mount. Therefore my advice is to all, except to that one man in fifty above mentioned, not to buy raw ponies, and, above all, not to begin to learn polo on a raw pony; for in this latter combination most assuredly will both pony and rider sink into the pit of failure. That one man who can train *any* pony to polo must be a man with perfect hands, seat, and, above all, temper; under his tuition raw ponies do indeed turn into gold. There is only one hint I can give him, as coming from one of the finest riders of the day: "When you feel that you are getting the least angry with a troublesome youngster, get off and walk home; in a moment of anger or impatience, you may do something which it will take you weeks of patient teaching to undo."

Be assured, there are more men who drop money on raw ponies than those who make a profit on them: their successes are few, their failures many. These being my sentiments, it is perhaps rather inconsistent to attempt to give any hints regarding the training of polo ponies; for I shall thereby feel partially guilty in aiding and abetting the following of a course which seems to me to be an unwise one for the majority of men to follow. However, as nothing I may say will probably deter the majority of men who do so now from buying in the rough in the future, I may as well do my best, with the aid of more experienced horsemen than myself, to give a few hints which may be useful to them.

In buying from dealers, it is necessary to be careful that you do not get an old "sahib's" pony, for ten to one it is a pony that has already proved a failure in some way. At the same time, if you know the pony and its history, and think it will suit you, you may very well use your superior knowledge in bargaining the dealer down to a reasonable figure, for there is no accusation a dealer will more stoutly deny than that his pony is a "sahib's" caster. "No, Sahib" (string of Mohammedan pious invocations), "I swear he came from a Zemindar of Shahpur only four days ago." It is necessary to be well up to dealers tricks too; and, as a safeguard against fraud, it is wise to insist on keeping his pony in your stables for a few days on trial. It is quite marvellous how, in the course of a single night, a dealer will transform a decrepit old crock into a sprightly youngster. Firstly, by doctoring his teeth, and, secondly, by putting a thick coating of wet clay on his legs. This latter device is especially ingenious, for during the bitterly cold night of a Punjab winter, the clay becomes as cold as death, and as it dries binds to the leg like a strait-waistcoat of ice; the result, from the close cold pressure, is that in the morning the pony's legs are as clean as a colt's. In buying from a dealer, never get a crowd of your friends to help you; nothing makes a dealer more angry and unapproachable than having his animals criticized by a lot of amateurs. Take him and his pony away quietly and, either alone or with the aid of one friend, talk the matter over with the owner. It is always wiser to gently argue rather than to get angry or insulting. When a dealer asks Rs. 300 for a pony, instead of saying "Pooh! he is not worth Rs. 150," it is more effective to mildly and politely disparage the pony, and pick it to pieces—to the dealer alone, of course, and not to a crowd of bystanders.

At a fair, I have known a zemindar take his mare away altogether, because a would-be purchaser got angry with him and applied abusive epithets to him because he would not sell at a reasonable price. A few days afterwards I met the man, and bought the mare at a much lower figure than the other gentleman had offered. I then asked him why he had not sold before at the fair, and his answer was—"That man, Sahib, was a devil; I am fond of the mare, and would not have let her pass into his hands for twice that money." Though we do not certainly find these soft traits in the dealer's character, yet, at the same time, it will always be found that a bargain courteously struck with him also will cost the purchaser less than buying from a wrathful and insulted owner. In buying straight from the zemindar, it is generally customary to use a go-between, who conducts the bargaining part of the business; either with the zemindar himself, or with one of his myrmidons, the two principals meanwhile chatting about indifferent matters.

I was much amused once, out in a village on the Yusufzai plain, when I was purchasing ponies from the villagers. The owner and I sat on charpoys and talked high politics, about the Amir of Kabul, the Russians, and what not: whilst our two "go-betweens" were bargaining together, and constantly referring to their principals in low whispers. The general conversation therefore ran much as follows:—

The Khan (*loq.*).—"Yes, your honour, I have heard that the Cossacks are not to be compared to our sowars, and [*in a low whisper to his 'go-between'* —'Say the mare cost me Rs. 200 only six months ago, and that I cannot let her go for less'] that they ride mere ponies instead of horses."

I (*loq.*).—"So I have heard [*a side whisper to my 'go-between'*—'Say I got a much better pony than that at the last village for Rs. 100; the same that Zafta Khan of Zeydah always rode'], but still they are great scouts, and have a great name in Europe."

And so on, both of us seeming to utterly ignore the matter on hand; which was finally settled to our mutual satisfaction by the "go-betweens," and the rupees paid by my man to the khan's.

In buying a raw pony, we can only be assured of three things—getting a sound animal, well shaped, and likely to turn out well. For the rest we have to trust to luck and the skill exhibited in training him. To judge of soundness, a man should be well up in the scientific part of the veterinary art; the rudiments of which can be gained by anyone of ordinary intelligence by a careful study of such clearly expressed and thoroughly professional books as Captain Hayes'. This book knowledge should be supplemented by applying his reading to practice, and by picking up wrinkles from old hands. For shape and make, beyond following the general rules to be found in veterinary books, it seems a good practical idea to get the likeness of the best pony of your acquaintance indelibly engraved on your memory, and with that likeness before you always to endeavour to buy an animal as nearly as possible shaped on those lines. Such ponies as Major G. Richardson's "Coquette," Hon. H. A. Lawrence's "Spark," Captain Bligh's "Victory," and Lieutenant C. Rich's "Voltigeur," are pattern ponies of different types. It was intended to give engravings of these ponies, but as it was found that photographs did not do justice to the animals, whereas drawings rather tended to idealize them, they have therefore been omitted.

Next, I come to "made" polo ponies. In buying

these, the ordinary purchaser is recommended to make soundness a first and indispensable condition. As before mentioned, where money is no object, it is open to the purchaser to make soundness entirely a secondary consideration to pace and play; for he can afford to pay for a luxury; and no luxury is more costly than a screw. The general purchaser, on the contrary, wants something that will last him some time, and which he can hope to sell without much loss when he goes on furlough. To these men, soundness in a pony is an all important factor; for without soundness, no animal can stand for long the severe strain required of it in playing the game of polo as at present played. It would be well, therefore, unless the purchaser is a practical judge of soundness, to call in the aid of a professional veterinary surgeon before buying a valuable pony. As regards shape and make, the purchaser has not the same difficulties to contend with as in buying ponies in the rough, for with a "made" pony we can almost afford to ignore make and shape; and after assuring ourselves of his soundness, we can proceed at once to examine him in the main requisities of a tournament pony—fastness, handiness, and knowledge of and aptitude for the game. Indian ponies, more than most breeds, run to all shapes and sizes; and it is never safe to condemn even the most miserable looking objects without actually trying them. I have known the most abject looking baggage pony rise to the dignity of playing in a tournament, and its price rise gradually from Rs. 50 to Rs. 500.

In buying a made pony, it is wise to take into consideration the man you are buying from, and his proficiency, or otherwise, at polo, his riding and weight. Under some men's hands, a pony steadily improves till it reaches a point as near perfection as its nature will allow; under others', on the contrary, it will steadily degenerate. It would be admissible to buy a pony from some men without ever even seeing it, in the assurance that their mounts are undoubtedly good; from others, it would be unwise to buy without trial. As to size, it is certainly not advisable to buy anything under a big 13-2 for tournament work, unless a perfectly phenomenal pony of smaller size is obtainable. Small ponies not only cannot, as a rule, hold their own in pace with large ones, but also in hustling weight must tell against them; added to this, there is the danger of being ridden down. Nothing is more appalling to a small pony and his rider than to see one of the modern leviathan ponies bearing down on him at full gallop; and nothing sickens a man more than to feel "out of it," owing to the smallness of his mount. Finally, never, if it can be avoided, buy from an advertisement, without first seeing the pony yourself; the advertiser writes in perfect good faith, no doubt, but he may see his own pony with partial eyes, and on purchasing him you may find that he is not at all that you expected.

Rather an instructive and, for outsiders, an amusing incident, regarding a pony bought from an advertisement, occurred the other day.

A young civilian down country, falling desperately in love with the advertised description of a pony in the *Pioneer*, telegraphed to the owner that he would take first refusal of the animal, and asked for further particulars by letter. In due course, the letter arrived. The pony was a "Bay; perfect polo pony and hack: played in several tournaments; carries a lady; broken to harness; perfectly sound; age 7 years; price, Rs. 500." A stiffish figure, but evidently worth the money, and he is telegraphed for accordingly.

About a week after, a syce (native groom) turns up with a bay pony, but as it has on a blanket and head-piece its form and shape are not visible.

"A real clipper though, I can see," says Jones, the happy purchaser.

Next morning, he orders the pony to be brought round for a short canter on the polo ground.

"Ha! hum! that 's rum; I had a sort of idea that the pony was a 'he,' but 'he' is evidently a 'she'—curious how one gets ideas into one's head without any rhyme or reason," remarks Jones to himself as he prepares to mount. "Walks remarkably well, and holds herself well. Here, syce, give me my polo stick. Whoa! there, old gal; don't be frightened. Never seen a polo stick in your life before, you old humbug—and you a veteran, who has played in several tournaments? Ha, ha! Excellent joke."

But joke or no joke, it took Jones half an hour to get hold of his stick, and when he had got it, the mare put her head down and went straight off into the country, regardless of every impediment which stood in her way, till a herd of cows crossing a bridge brought her up in a heap, but only because she failed to jump the crowd.

"A bit fresh after her railway journey, no doubt; must be rather hard to turn, though, at polo."

Next day, Mrs. Jones was to take the new pony for a short canter in the morning; and, in the afternoon, Jones proposed electrifying the station on his new polo pony. He did; but of that more anon.

Mrs. Jones came back very hot and cross, and ready to bet her best bonnet that the pony had never seen a lady's habit in its life before, much less carried one. At first it spun round like a teetotum, in mortal fear of the onesided-looking black skirt, and then proceeded to try and rub it off against every tree and wall in the station. No wonder Mrs. Jones was cross and angry, for the pony had finally laid itself down in the dust, with a view to rolling, whereupon Mrs. Jones hopped off, and had to walk home with the pony.

In the afternoon Jones took the pony down to polo.

"She will be all right with other ponies. Not accustomed to go about alone, my dear."

She certainly was fond of other ponies, and having got well amongst them, proceeded to dispense a few good-natured kicks indiscriminately around. When the game first began she seemed quite to like it, and frolicked about with the rest of the ponies; a joyous, playful little thing. After about three minutes, though, she had had enough of it, and fond thoughts of home and gram floated through her brain. No sooner thought of than acted upon, and absolutely regardless of the crowd that lined the touch-line, she dashed through it; knocked one man senseless, stampeded a pony-trap with a lady sitting in it, and nearly decapitating Jones in a low door-way, dashed into her stable.

On the spur of the moment, and fired with an excusable feeling of wrath, Jones sat down and wrote a few warm words to the former owner of the pony, and requested back his money and also to be relieved of the pony.

By return of post he received a quiet and dignified refusal; the character of the pony, as before given, was reiterated, and backed up by the testimony of two independent witnesses who had seen the pony play excellently in tournaments. The letter ended with a dubious reference to Jones's equestrian powers.

So Jones had to consume his wrath, and keep the pony.

Months afterwards, a friend was lunching with him who had known the pony in former days, and after lunch asked to see it again.

He had no sooner set eyes on it than he exclaimed—

"Why, that's not the pony I mean! He was a gelding, I know, and that is a mare!"

To make a long story short, after a lot of writing and hard swearing, it was discovered that the same pony that had been despatched had not been the one to reach Jones; in fact, an exchange had been made on the way down country, and Jones's Rs. 500 pony had been swopped for a worthless mare. The original syce who had done this exceedingly smart trick had meanwhile taken his discharge, and could never be traced again. Jones has never again bought from an advertisement without seeing his purchase first; and I advise you to follow his example.

CHAPTER IV.

HINTS ON TRAINING A POLO PONY.

WE will now give a few notes on the training of a polo pony. See, first, that your mount is comfortably and suitably bitted, and that his saddle fits comfortably; then use him for hacking work only, till both you and he are perfectly accustomed to each other and perfect friends. With many ponies, this preliminary training will require a month, and sometimes more; with others, on the contrary, a few days' hacking will be found sufficient. The rider must be the judge as to when he and his pony are at complete accord. During this period of hacking, it is well to gradually introduce a polo stick; at first, merely holding it quietly, and afterwards, if it is seen that the animal is not afraid of it, gently whirling it round and round on both sides; very great care being taken that the pony is not accidentally hit by it. Having got him quite accustomed to the stick, get a ball and knock it about quietly at a walk for a couple of hours a day, until he follows it without showing any signs of fear. The next step is to teach him to be handy and quick at turning, firstly, by circling him small to right and left, and also describing a figure of 8 in a riding school; secondly, by starting him off short splits and easing up, then turning sharp round and cantering sharp back again; again turning and repeating the manœuvre, till the pony quite understands what is required of him, viz. to start sharp into a gallop, to pull up at any moment, turn on his own axis, and go back on the same line at a gallop. Having at the end of a month or six weeks got so far in his education, next canter him after the ball, at first straight ahead, and then interspersing a few backhanders at intervals. The rider would do well to avoid trying fancy strokes till later in the pony's training, for he is very apt to hit his pony in executing them, and a slight hit makes a more lasting impression on a youngster's memory than dozens of hits on an old polo pony's. When he is quite steady and handy, the pony may be galloped about near a game, carrying an umpire, for instance, for a few minutes at a time. Next, he may be taken into a game, for a few minutes only at first; his period of play being gradually increased, till he can play the full time which will be required of him without getting excited and out of hand. As before stated, it is impossible to fix exactly the length of time required for training a pony, because ponies vary so much in temperament, docility, and aptitude; but it may be generally stated that a pony should not be taken into a game under three months' training. The first great essential to success, more especially in the earlier phases of a pony's education, is to keep him steadily at it day after day, and not to train him spasmodically. The second is *never* to get angry with him. If you find wrath arising in your bosom, just dismount and walk home. It is, as often as not, your fault that things are going wrong and not the pony's, for a pony does not smoke strong cigars nor drink a multitude of pegs, and, consequently, he does not wake up on a scorching morning with a mouth like an ashpit, and a head seething and aching to the splitting point; whereas, you may possibly have done all these things.

Such, briefly, is a pretty sure way of effectively training a polo pony—given fair hands, fair seat, and all-abiding patience.

As touched on in a former chapter, the matter of shape, in other words physical adaptability to the game, is a very important factor in the training of a polo pony. Putting aside for a moment all questions of temper and temperament, it will be manifest to the least observant that a pony which is so constructed physically as to be in a position to best fulfil the duties required of it at polo, will naturally be an apter pupil than one in which nature has placed some physical deformity which stands in the way of its educational progress. Take a U-necked pony, for instance. The head and neck are the rudder by which we guide, with the aid of the reins, our pony through the narrow intricacies of the game; if that steering gear is so malformed as to be nearly useless, it is manifest that we shall be unable to guide our pony properly, and shall therefore find him unplayable at polo, where so much depends upon handiness. Again, take a bull-necked, heavy-shouldered beast, all "down in the bows," to borrow a seafaring term, it is evident he is not constructed to take a light and active part in life, polo is not his profession, any more than riding steeplechases is that of an alderman of London. No doubt, with time and patience, we could teach the latter to ride steeplechases and the former to play polo, but the game seems scarcely worth the candle. It seems absurd to say so, but even men who rather fancy themselves as judges, in the hurry of concluding what they think a smart bargain, fail to notice the U-neck or heavy shoulder in the smart-looking, prancing pony which the dealer on his back holds together with such consummate skill. There is, again, the long snake-like necked animal, with so long and pliable a neck, indeed, that it doubles its chin up to its chest and goes whither it listeth completely controlless. There is, too, the flat-sided "herring-gutted" animal, which we may predict with confidence is short of wind and deficient, in consequence, in staying powers. Above all to be avoided is the fiddle-headed, roman-nosed animal, for that always denotes a hard-mouthed, hopeless puller. Avoid like a pestilence the very faintest inclination towards a roman nose; the taint is assuredly there, and will develop itself before you have had your pony very long. We are not attempting here to give all the physical defects that occur in pony-kind, but only a few of those prominent and leading ones which are likely to stand very materially in our way in training a pony to play polo. Nor do we wish any man who happens to possess a pony with the above disqualifications to immediately cast his pony as useless; but, rather, we will attempt to aid him in his task by enumerating a few old and well-known methods of obviating as much as possible the effect of these deficiencies. A U-necked pony, as all the world knows, is a pony with a U neck; that is, his crest, instead of being arched, takes the opposite or U curve. The anatomical result is that the animal's nose is thrown into the air, and we find it impossible to get a proper bearing on his mouth; in fact, our steering gear, as before mentioned, is out of order. The first object to be attained towards obviating the evil is evidently to get his nose down into the proper position. A running martingale is no good, and an ordinary standing martingale is little better; the sovereign remedy is a "Cheshire" martingale, and if that will not act nothing else that we know of will. Cheshire martingales are not very generally known, and therefore we will describe one, but before doing so we would draw attention to the fact that, rightly or wrongly, we consider that a U neck in a horse, just like a round back in a child, can be made or cured whilst either are young. We have seen a series of horses and ponies grow U necked from hard work, with a heavy weight up whilst very young, and we have seen young U-necked horses completely cured of their deformity.

A Cheshire martingale is constructed like an ordinary running martingale, with one very important difference. In the place of the two rings through which the reins pass in a running martingale, we have two swivels which hook on to the rings of the snaffle on either side. That is the principle; in construction it is neater to have one long strap coming from the girth, which close to the mouth ends in two short lengths of chain with a swivel at the end of each. With the aid of a buckle, which should be about half way between the chin and the girth, the martingale can, after being adjusted, be tightened down to the required length. It would seem, theoretically, that this is a very violent and drastic remedy, and that the animal with his head bound down in this to him unnatural position, would be incapable of activity or rapid motion. Practically, however, it is far otherwise; a horse "gives" to it at once, and the rider has gained his object of getting his horse's head into the right position. The great advantage of this martingale, too, is its adaptability to the hunting field; it is the only martingale which is at once effective and perfectly safe. Even a horse quite strange to one will in an hour or two get accustomed to it, and will take his jumps without any of that danger to himself and his rider which is attendant on jumping a horse in an ordinary standing martingale. The Cheshire martingale is of course equally useful for "staring" horses, who carry their noses in the air and do not look where they are going.

The opposite extreme to the U-necked pony is the animal with the very long and thin neck, which makes the steering gear ineffective by doubling its chin up to its chest. Clearly, an opposite remedy is required for this class; we want to keep his nose up and out a bit, instead of down and in. The American trotting-horse bearing-rein is perhaps better than the ordinary English bearing-rein for effecting this purpose. The American variety is fitted as follows: A thin round rein is attached to the centre of the pommel of the saddle, and running along the crest of the animal's neck, passes through a ring between his ears, and continuing on to the forehead there splits in two, the two straps then running down to the rings of the snaffle on either side. It is at once apparent that thereby a physically impassable barrier is placed in the way of the pony getting his head in too much. Very nice hands, temper, and judgment are required to make anything out of a pony with this strap on.

For the heavy necked animal, if a stallion, we can only recommend gelding. A gelding's neck often fines down to a wonderful extent, and may be helped towards improvement by heavy sweating clothes, but few ponies are worth the trouble and risk. By the way, in gelding, one of the results is that the animal as a rule no longer has a glossy coat in winter, but grows a thick coarse one; it is noticeable, however, that horses gelt in the spring never carry such coarse coats as those gelt in the autumn.

A roman-nosed, apparently hopeless puller may, and is very often quite brought to his bearings by a gag net. The net fits fairly close over his mouth and nostrils, and the reins are attached to rings at each side of it. By tightening the reins the mouth and nostrils are closed, and our puller is obliged to come up all standing, for want of breath. This method is neither inhuman nor in any way hard on the horse, and he generally takes to it very kindly. For a pony, too, which may suffer from diseased teeth or jaws, and to whom a bit is mortal agony, a net is comfort and joy.

For the flat-sided, herring-gutted pony, we can suggest no remedy, his is a physical deformity which art cannot mitigate or overcome.

CHAPTER V.

ON POLO STICKS.

On the subject of sticks, there is a great variety of opinion; nearly every regiment has heads or handles of different patterns. Taking "heads" the first, there are, generally speaking, the following varieties:—

(1.) The cylindrical shape: made of ash, sheeshum, or some other hard and comparatively heavy wood. Diameter generally about 2 inches, length about 9 inches. These heads have the advantage of driving well, and cover an inch or two more ground laterally than most heads. On the other hand, they are heavy and tiring, and on a bumpy ground, are more likely to cut under the ball than heads of greater bulk.

(2.) The flat-sided, boat-shaped head: this, too, is generally made of rather heavy, close-grained woods, but it is a safer hitting shape than the first described; at the same time, it loses an inch or two of lateral sweep.

(3.) The cylindrical shape: made of willow, or other very light wood, and as big as a croquet mallet head. This head combines great hitting power with lightness and durability.

(4.) The round-sided, boat-shaped willow head: with a great thickness of wood where the stick pierces it, and tapering off towards the ends. This seems to be a generally favourite stick, though apparently it has no advantages over No. 3, except, possibly, additional lightness.

There are several methods of fixing on the heads:—

(1.) By pushing the cane through the hole in the head, slightly splitting the cane that protrudes, and driving in a wedge; the projecting end then being sawed off.

(2.) By boring a transverse hole through head and cane, and driving an iron or wooden peg through the hole.

(3.) First, securely nail a rim of leather round the head of the cane, leaving the upper edge of it, *i.e.* the edge which is towards the handle, flapping loose. Push the cane, leather and all, through the hole in the head, and then draw it back, when it will be found that the loose edge of the leather rim will turn inside out, and thereby securely jam the cane in the head. A transverse peg may be driven through for additional security.

(4.) By having all your canes shod with light brass ferules, through which a transverse hole is bored. The head is then fitted on, and an iron screw or rivet driven through.

This last method will be found the best and most durable; for however many heads you may break or lose, a new one can be fixed on in a moment, without, as is usually the case, having to cut off an inch of cane before driving a new hole for the peg. It is advisable to bind the bottom six inches of the cane, from the head upwards, with fine, strong, waxed thread; and some men connect this with another bandage of the same string, which goes round the head also, and securely lashes the two together. Others, instead of string, have a leather case which fits round the bottom of the stick and the head, and binds them together. It must be remembered, however, that each of these methods, though affording additional security, adds also to the weight of the stick, leather especially so.

The length of stick varies according to the taste and fancy of the player. A good length of stick for most people is when the head of the stick just touches the ground when held in the right hand, the holder being mounted. When an owner has two or three ponies of different heights, he should have sticks made of suitable length for each pony, or he will find that on changing from a small pony to a big one, using the same length stick, that he will be constantly missing the ball from hitting over it; and, *vice versa*, in changing from a big pony on to a small one, he will find that he constantly hits the ground two or three inches behind the ball. It may be added that the actual height in inches of a pony, standing still, will not always be a safe standard whereby to regulate the shortening or lengthening of the stick; for often a small pony with a high, round, galloping action will require as long a stick as a taller pony with a low smooth gallop.

There is only one kind of polo cane in ordinary use in India, and that is the rattan, which varies only in the length of its joints according to the climate in which it grows. The Neilgherry cane is generally considered the best.

Handles are of two kinds—round and flat; of these, the latter are generally considered the safest and best. With them there is no danger of the stick turning in one's hand at a critical moment, nor is there a chance of discovering (at the moment of hitting) that one is not hitting with the head fair and square to the front. Either cord, or *nawar*,* or leather, are generally used to bind round the handle,

* Indian cotton webbing.

and a loop for the wrist is frequently used as a safeguard against accidentally dropping the stick. I have heard this latter described as a dangerous custom, on the grounds that your stick may catch in something, or somebody going in another direction, and that you may thereby be hauled off your pony; but during the last ten years of polo we have neither seen nor heard of an authenticated case of such an accident happening. I think, therefore, I may safely recommend those who find their sticks are liable to slip out of their hands to make a practice of wearing wrist loops. Many men soak their polo-stick heads in water before playing, others oil them; the effect, in both cases, being to make the head fit tighter on to the stick. Though additional security is obtained by this method, extra weight is also added.

It will often be found that canes that have been kept unused for any length of time in a hot or dry climate become very brittle and unreliable. To put these canes into working order again, it is necessary to introduce oil or moisture into the fibres. This is best done by fixing on to one end of each cane an empty Martini-Henry cartridge-case with the butt end cut off; fill this with oil, and leave the cane standing upright for a few days until the oil has been absorbed. It will be found that, the cartridge-case being of metal, merely the pressure of the thumb will be sufficient to embed the case in the cane sufficient securely for the purpose required. The narrow end of the cartridge-case is the end which should be embedded in the cane.

Speaking generally, perhaps the main evil to guard against is having sticks too heavy for the strength of the player. In polo, as in cricket, many a man loses a great proportion of his handiness, and misses the ball more frequently than he ought to, through having sticks whose weight it is beyond his strength to wield effectively.

CHAPTER VI.

REGIMENTAL POLO CLUBS.

It may be of interest to those who have not yet started Regimental Polo Clubs, and who are anxious to do so, to learn what several systems have been tried by different regiments, and with what success. The subject of Station Polo Clubs need not be entered upon here, for their finances are regulated on the simple basis of providing a polo ground, balls, &c., at the lowest possible rate of subscription. A regimental polo club has, on the contrary, many difficult and complicated financial problems to solve before it can put a good team into the field. The main object of regimental clubs is to save the members of the team, and the officers of the regiment generally, from feeling too severely at one time the pecuniary strain which would, without this provision, fall upon them on entering for a tournament. As far as I have been able to learn, there are at present three methods of running a polo club now in vogue amongst regiments serving in India.

Firstly, there are those clubs which are worked on the system of having club ponies—that is, ponies purchased out of the club funds for the use of the members of the team and others. The club also pays for all tournament and out-station match expenses, and for the feed and keep of the club ponies. It also advances money to officers for the purchase of polo ponies; refund being made by monthly instalments of Rs. 50.

In the second category may be placed those clubs which are entirely money clubs, and which do not own club ponies. Their object is to advance money to individual members for the purchase of approved ponies; refund being taken by easy instalments. The club also pays all out-station match and tournament expenses.

Thirdly, there are those clubs which confine themselves entirely to defraying the expenses of out-station matches and tournaments, and which do not either buy club ponies or lend money to members for their purchase.

Of these three systems, the third is, of course, the cheaper for non-playing members; but expense falls very heavily on the regimental team, who have to mount themselves without any aid from the regiment.

The first system is, taken all round, the most expensive, unless worked with considerable skill and luck; the skill and luck coming in in the purchase of raw ponies, which, after being carefully trained, rise enormously in value, and can be sold for the profit of the club, either to members of the club or to outsiders, according to circumstances. Personally, I am rather against this system of having club ponies, after having seen it given a very fair trial for several years. This on the grounds that a club pony is no particular person's property, and very possibly is not ridden twice in a fortnight by the same rider; the consequence being that a pony, unless it is a very old stager, gets into all sorts of bad ways. It is most necessary at polo for rider and pony to be in complete accord, and though we often take upon ourselves to decide that a certain club pony suits Jones but does not suit Robinson, we often forget to consider whether the pony on his part also agrees with us in thinking Jones a more suitable and friendly man to play with than Robinson. Again, Brown has one way of communicating his wishes on a certain point to his pony; Jones another, and Robinson another. If either one of the three rode the pony regularly, the animal would very soon understand what was wanted of him; but when all three are taking turn and turn about on him, the poor pony loses all patience, gives up trying to please, probably shows temper, and is immediately voted a bad pony by all three riders, and cast accordingly. With regard to the purchase of club ponies, the system in vogue is for the club to buy ponies either in the rough, or trained, up to a certain limited number, varying generally from six to twelve.

When this number is exceeded, owing to the purchase of fresh ponies, the surplus number are offered for sale, either in or out of the regiment, at a price fixed by the polo club committee, according to the market value of polo ponies at the time, members of the regiment being probably given a preference at a lower rate, and the price being recovered in easy instalments from them. The club ponies are either stabled all together and placed under the supervision of a non-commissioned officer, or else, to save expenses, they are billeted about in the different officers' stables, or in the troop lines; and a couple of rupees a month extra pay is given to the officer's or non-commissioned officer's syce who looks after each pony. All the arrangements for the grass and grain for the club ponies is most carefully made, grain being bought and grass stacked when rates are lowest, so as to tide over bad times, and to save as much as posssible the finances of a club.

The remaining system, the second of those enumerated above—that of making the club a purely money club—appears to us to be, on the whole, the best. The club runs no risk of loss in ponies, nor does it have to stand the cost of the feed and keep of the club ponies and their attendants. At the same time, it is always prepared to advance money, without interest, for the purchase by individuals of ponies approved of by the committee as likely to be suitable for playing in a tournament. As these loans are recoverable, the actual expenses of the club are limited to paying for the railing of the ponies to tournaments and a few incidental expenses which may be incurred in connection with out-station matches. The tournament expenses will, of course, vary according to the distance the competitors are by rail from the place where the tournament is to be held; but, taken one year with another, Rs. 500 per annum ought to cover the expenses incurred by a regimental team at a tournament.

To successfully float a club of this sort, every officer on joining should pay an entrance fee of Rs. 50, and all officers a monthly subscription of Rs. 10. When the club is fairly under way, and has accumulated a certain amount of capital, the monthly subscription can be reduced. If the club is at any time wound up, each member will get back his share of the capital in hand, which should be, if the club has been well-managed, something over and above his entrance-fee.

CHAPTER VII.

EN ROUTE TO A TOURNAMENT.

PONIES can be conveyed by rail to a tournament either in cattle-trucks or horse-boxes, a single fare being charged for the return journey. A cattle-truck will hold twelve ponies, and a horse-box six; so that the cost of conveyance in trucks will be very considerably less than in horse-boxes; but, at the same time, it must be remembered that in a cattle-truck the ponies are more or less loose and liable to injury, and that it is imprudent to carry stallions and mares in the same truck. In a horse-box, on the contrary, each pony has his own compartment, and is comfortably bolstered up on all sides, with a manger to feed out of, and a trap-door for the removal of dung. Moreover, the railway companies undertake no responsibility for ponies travelling in a cattle-truck, whereas they are liable for an accident happening to ponies in a horse-box. On the whole, therefore, it would seem advisable to use horse-boxes, at any rate, for the most valuable ponies in a team.

Talking of horse-boxes reminds us of a very ingenious method of inducing, or rather compelling, an unwilling pony to enter a horse-box, or, indeed, to do anything else, to which he has a frivolous objection, immediately and without a moment's delay. The method was shown us by Captain Hayes, in his horse-breaking lectures, and for effective simplicity beats any other method that we have come across. We have all, most probably, at one time or another in our careers found ourselves fuming about the platform of a railway station and uttering perchance strange oaths because one refractory pony, after all the others are in, will not enter the horse-box; we have tried everything, from blandishments and twitches down to a tandem whip and abusive epithets on him, without avail; we have even tried the old rope trick familiar to the railway official, with the oft repeated results, that just as we have begun to congratulate ourselves on having at last successfully crowded him into his box, he turns sharp round and stares blankly—if not defiantly—at us, with the rope across his chest instead of round his rump. Captain Hayes' method is neither cruel nor complicated, and acts on the anatomical principle that when we can appeal to an animal along his spine our arguments are irresistible; they do not hurt, but they are, all the same, irresistible. The method and its application are as follows:—Take a length of rope eight or nine yards long—a pair of the ordinary heel-ropes in use in the East will do—and, doubling it, make a rough crupper by tying a knot close to the doubled end. Slip this crupper over the pony's tail, and run the two loose ends of rope forward, one on each side of him, first passing them under the flaps of the saddle and next through the rings of the snaffle; or if the pony is unsaddled, under the roller and through the rings of the watering bridle. The operator then stands in front of the pony, and taking one of the slack ends of the rope in each hand, simply pulls the pony into the box as easily as if he were a child. We have him right along the spine, and his power of resistance is absolutely *nil.* He cannot even resort to passive resistance, by laying back his weight and refusing to move; he must go forward, and at the same time his forehand is left free for action. For one man to try to pull a horse into a box or across a ditch by main force with a rope attached to his head is, of course, as hopeless a task as it would be to pull a house across the street; but using the above described method, a man may stand on one side of a ditch and the heaviest horse created on the other, and in a tug-of-war between the two the man is bound to prevail, and that immediately.

The ponies should arrive at their destination several days before the tournament begins, for many ponies are completely upset by a long railway journey, and would be quite out of form if immediately played in a game. Arrangements for grass to be stacked and grain collected should have been made well in advance, so that everything may be found ready on arrival. It is advisable that both ponies and men should play once, at least, on a strange ground before the tournament commences, so as to get into the ways of the ground, and to feel their legs generally.

A short paragraph on shoeing, though only indirectly connected with polo, might not be amiss here. It is better, on the whole, if a pony's feet will stand it, not to shoe him at all for polo; and there are few ponies which require more than shoeing in front, the hind hoofs being left in a state of nature. Just as boots detract somewhat from the activity and sure-footedness of mankind, so we are inclined to think do shoes from those of a pony. Just hammering along a road, both boots to a man and shoes to a pony are neither in the way or incommodious; but when we get off the road, and a little activity or sure-footedness is required, the man takes off his boots and puts on running-shoes or indiarubber-soled shoes or grass-shoes, according to the form of exercise he is about to take; and a pony would in the same way no doubt, if we could get his own opinion on the subject, inform us that he could play polo much better without shoes than with them. Of course, many pony's fore feet will not stand the work without shoes, and even those whose feet will stand it must be accustomed gradually to the change; but there are very few ponies which cannot be played without shoes on their hind feet, straight away. To jump to the opposite extreme, some grounds in India are so hard that to play on them is nearly as severe a strain on a pony's legs and feet as if he were playing on an ordinary turnpike road. For play on these grounds, therefore, it will be found advisable to use habitually concussion pads in shoeing all ponies. A concussion pad being a strip of leather or india-rubber which, following the shape of the shoe, acts as a pad between it and the hoof, and takes off greatly from the heavy jar to which legs and feet are subject every time the foot comes to the ground in galloping.

As this chapter seems to be made up more or less of odds and ends, perhaps the worthy umpire—not that we wish to insult him by calling him either an odd or an end—may as well find a place here as elsewhere. It goes without saying that the umpires—there are always two—must be proficient in their knowledge of the game in all its latest developments, and that they must be well mounted and keep their eyes very wide open. There is no game which it is more difficult to umpire in satisfactorily than in a game of polo. If the umpire is too close to the game, he gets in the way of the players; if too far off, he falls into the opposite error of being not near enough to judge on close differences of opinion that may arise. There are at present, to the best of our knowledge, no definite instructions laid down for an umpire's use beyond the broad suggestion that he shall acquaint himself with the rules, and that he shall judge accordingly. There are many points which have arisen, and probably will arise again in connection with an umpire and his duties, which very possibly require to be legislated for. For instance, supposing the ball in its career towards perhaps a prospective goal hits an umpire or his pony, what then? At present, as nothing is to be made out of it, it is considered unwise to hit the umpire more than necessary, as calculated to make him angry and biassed against the hitter; and any rule which is made on this subject will, it is evident, have so to be framed as to discountenance players pursuing the umpire with a view to hitting him and claiming a foul over the job. Again, supposing one umpire gives one verdict and the other an entirely contrary one on a certain point that may be raised. What is to happen? Shall we split the difference, or shall we go by what the nearest umpire says, or shall we listen to neither and go on with the game? We have seen all three alternatives resorted to on different occasions.

Again, a man claims a foul, but play is not stopped unless one of the umpires happens to be close up, and has lungs sufficiently strong to make his verdict heard. Meanwhile the gentleman who claimed the foul has perforce galloped off with a grievance at his heart, which naturally affects his play for the next minute or two, half his attention being on the game and half on trying to make out whether the umpire has decided for or against him. A simple remedy, which we have often seen recommended but not tried, though we believe it is customary in some parts of India, is to provide each umpire with a small red hand flag, which he is instructed to hold aloft whenever he allows a foul, taking no notice whatever of claims to fouls which he does not consider such. Directly the red flag is held up a trumpeter, who is stationed next the time-keeper on the touch-line sounds the "Halt," or "Cease firing," and the game comes immediately to a stand-still; for those players who may not see the red flag, at any rate hear the trumpet.

Another nondescript matter, which may well be included in a nondescript chapter, is the matter of "colours"; we refer more particularly to "colours" worn in ordinary scratch station games. It is customary, in India, either to make no distinction between the two sides—which makes confusion worse confounded, more especially if players are constantly cutting in and out, as is usual in a station game—or else cloth cross belts of red and blue are provided for the two sides; but even this distinction is often not decided enough to eliminate mistakes in the hurry and scurry and dust of a fast game. In Malta and Egypt, a much better plan used to exist. Each player owns two very thin, gauzelike jockey shirts made of some cheap material, the one red and the other blue. These he takes always down to the polo ground with him as part of his turn-out, and when the sides are made up he just slips on the red or blue shirt as the case may be over his jersey and a marked and unmistakable distinction between the sides is at once established. If any changes in the composition of the sides takes place during the afternoon, those changed over change their shirts also.

Our inexorable publisher still writes "this chapter wants adding to." What on earth are we to add? It has grown already, under severe pressure, from one page to its present dimensions; we know nothing more about polo, and a treatise on the "Higher Culture of the Nineteenth Century" will not be completely *apropos*. A great number of amusing and improving anecdotes on every other subject that the mind of man can imagine, except polo occur to our mind immediately. We feel sorely tempted to follow the example of a certain friend of ours, who was up for the Staff College examination. His weak point was French, and his instructor had, with eminent forethought, considered it necessary to make him learn up spontaneous-looking essays on every subject that was likely to be set, such as Boulanger, the Eiffel Tower, the Panama Canal, the Volunteers. The examiners, however, with equally commendable forethought, carefully avoided asking for an essay on any of the prominent topics of the day, demanding instead a treatise on the "*rôle* of cavalry in campaigns of the future." An ordinary mortal would have been completely defeated but not so our friend. His essay, translated literally, commenced: "Monsieur the examiner, with regret the most profound, I have the misfortune to inform you that I know not anything of the subject 'the *rôle* of cavalry in campaigns of the future'; but——" and then he proceeded to deliver himself of a long and interesting essay, in which he skilfully combined all he had learnt about Boulanger, the Eiffel Tower, the Panama Canal, and the Volunteers. Need it be added that such genius had its reward, and that that officer passed in French, the examiners remark on the subject being: "No. 1,052 has just secured the qualifying number of marks; but he appears to have mistaken"—gentle sarcasm—"the subject set for the essay." In the same way, we feel irresistibly inclined to write "We know nothing more about polo; but it is a well known fact that Napoleon I., &c. &c.," giving an epitomized account of the rise and fall of that great man, up to the required number of pages. But that course would perhaps be open to reproof from the powers above, and therefore, by way of sticking to our subject, it might not be out of place to give a short account of a lady's polo match, which took place—where and when we are bound, under the most solemn vows, never to reveal. The match was between four married ladies and four single ones, each side being allowed one of the opposite and more brutal sex to act as a support and back-bone to the team; but it was specially ordained that neither of them was to go up into the game and hit the ball about too much, or hustle in an unladylike manner.

The game was a very fast and good one for about a minute, and then one of the unmarried ladies called a halt, on the ground that her veil was dreadfully in the way, and she really must take it off—which she accordingly did, whilst everyone waited—and the male member of the team was called up and ordered to put it in his pocket: an unreasonable and even tyrannical request when made to a man with next to no clothing on, and certainly no pockets in it.

Another minute of stern and businesslike play—during which the two teams managed to hit the ball three distinct times between them—and then Mrs. A. declared she could play no longer with gloves on, because she could not hold her stick properly; and Mrs. B. having played so far without gloves, taking the opposite view, said she could play no longer without gloves, and that her rings hurt her dreadfully. So these two went off to the touch line, the one to take off her gloves and the other to put them on. This was a famous opportunity for all the rest of the party to discover that something or other was wrong with them, their ponies, or their get up. Having soothed and set straight everything and everybody, the two males get off their ponies, light cigars, and sit down on the ground to await the development of affairs. After a quarter of an hour's rest they developed into another three minutes' play, during which a considerable improvement in the all-round play was noticeable, and one of the males hit a goal for his side much to the indignation of all the ladies on the other side. Then followed two more minutes' play, during which the other male, incited thereto by the reproofs liberally administered to him by his own side, hit a corresponding goal for them. By the nature of things, it was now in the ordinary course of events, tea time, and an adjournment for this necessary meal was at once decided upon. After tea, which occupied one way or another about half an hour, play was resumed; everyone seemed greatly revived, and some really good runs were made. It is quite astonishing what wonders tea works on the female constitution; a crowded drawing-room is still as the grave till tea is introduced, but the bare sight of a muffin and cup of tea sets the whole place in an uproar, if one may use such a phrase when speaking of the silvery organs of the gentler sex. So in our game tea made all the difference, and the play afterwards was really astonishingly good considering the inexperience of the players. Having the off-side of the pony quite clear, they could get a clean hit on that side, and those on handy, well-trained ponies appeared to be very nearly as active after the ball as men would be. As long as ladies play only in a ladies' game, and ride handy, well-trained ponies, there is no reason why polo should not, like hunting, become a pastime for our sisters and cousins and aunts as well as for ourselves. To return to our match: after in all about twenty minutes play, it was voted that the game should be declared drawn, everyone being too hot and tired to go on.

There, that is all, and we could not add another line to this chapter even if placed at the business end of a loaded double-barrel shot gun, and gently urged to do so under pain of instant dissolution.

CHAPTER VIII.

POLO TOURNAMENTS.

WITH regard to polo tournaments in India, perhaps the following notes may be of use to those who have never yet entered for a tournament, and whose ambition it is to do so. "Rome was not built in a day"; and, to compare small things with great, nor is a polo team. The winning team in a tournament is generally the outcome of years of training, years of expense, and years spent in the selection of men and of ponies. "It is as easy for a camel to go through the eye of a needle" as for four individually good players to win a tournament from a disciplined team. All, then, a new team can hope for, during the first few years of its existence, is just to keep its head above water, and, perhaps, even to get through the first ties of a tournament. Then, as confidence grows, as year by year indifferent ponies are weeded out and good ones take their places, as feelings of mutual support and reliance amongst the members of the team are developed, so, in corresponding proportion, that team rises in the polo world. Between a very inferior team and a middling good one is an enormous, unspeakable gap of comparison; between a middling team and a first-class one is but a little step, up which it is possible to step in a few months. we refer, of course, to teams of the same *genus*, so to speak, and in the same category; for it would be absurd, judging by actual historical facts, to say that a second-class station team, for instance, could in a few months rise to the level of the winners of the Open Cavalry Tournament. What we want to lay stress on is the difficulty of beginning; once mediocrity is reached, the rest must come with a little perseverance, and may come with a bound.

It is, perhaps, worth noting that hitherto it has almost invariably been a regiment which has put in a long period of Indian service which has won the open Cavalry or Infantry tournaments, and no case has yet occurred of a regiment new, or comparatively new, to the country winning either. In the same way, almost invariably an old and seasoned team wins the Native Cavalry Tournament. A young team should not, therefore, be disheartened because it does not win straight away; let it but use the experience it gains, year after year, and it may rest assured that its time will come. Bearing this in mind, it would be unwise for a new team to rush into violent expense in the matter of ponies; and nothing will cripple and, perhaps, ruin the finances of a polo club more speedily than buying up made ponies at fabulous prices, at the last moment, before a tournament. Rather buy steadily and gradually, as chances offer, building up your team pony by pony in a wise and business-like manner. All failures should be immediately cast, and sold to the best advantage, for a good pony eats no more than a bad one; and the "failure" is an institution which in most regiments seems to hang on indefinitely. It is better to make the plunge, and sell at a considerable loss, than to go on feeding a useless mouth for months and sometimes years, on the chance of selling well. How often do we see forty or even fifty ponies belonging to a regiment, out of which number it is most difficult to find eighteen fit to play in a tournament! Now, instead of keeping on that crowd of twenty or thirty useless ponies, would it not be wiser, from the owner's point of view, and also to the general interest of the regiment, if, instead of useless ponies, each man kept one or two ponies fit to play in the regimental team. Some will at once exclaim, "Oh, but I can't afford to buy a pony up to tournament form." Believe us, if you only bide your time, and buy with discretion, you will get an animal which is fit to play in the regimental team, and yet whose initial cost is not a rupee more than that of the three-legged old screw you are at present keeping. The senior officers in regiments and regimental doctors, all of whom draw high pay, can, with little or no extra expense to themselves, keep ponies fit to play in any tournament.

It is, as we say, a self-evident fact that a good pony will eat no more and cost no more to keep than a bad one, and his initial cost will, if the pony is bought with judgment, be merely money invested; for a good pony will always fetch his price anywhere. Of course, accidents will happen, and ponies will get screwed occasionally, but that is the fortune of war; and, we imagine, few men in the position of those we have mentioned would grudge the loss if entailed by fair wear and tear and for the good of their regiments. To young officers the loss might be serious, and no doubt arrangements could be made by which they would be entitled to some compensation from the polo club fund.

Simultaneously with the selection and training of the ponies, a like process should be going on with regard to the men who are to compose the team. Certain men show a certain aptitude for certain places in the game, and it is manifestly right to play men in the places that suit then. The "places," of course, are "back," "No. 3," "No. 2," and "No. 1," or "flying man," or, as they are sometimes named, "back," "two half-backs," and a "forward." It is only when certain problems arise that we can offer any advice. For instance, a regiment may contain three very good "backs," and no one else worth anything. Or it may have a plethora of "flying men," or two or three "No. 2's," and so on. It will, we think, be conceded that the two best all-round men should play "back" and "No. 2" respectively, for these two are the most important places in the game. Of these two, if there is no special aptitude shown by either for "back," the best all-round man of the two should be put there; for we think it will be conceded that "back" is the most important man in the team, both offensively and defensively, and more especially in the latter *rôle*, for no position requires greater nerve, resolution, and pluck than to play "back," for instance, in a losing game. The best ponies, too, should, on these grounds, go to the "back"; for without the best of mounts he is unnecessarily handicapped, and, in the presence of a "No. 1" mounted on superior ponies he will find it impossible to hold his own or guard his goal. It used to be an old-fashioned idea that you must put your *heaviest* man "back," and your *lightest* "No. 1." This idea was exploded by a series of light-weight "backs," superbly mounted, who played right up in the game, and turned the *rôle* of "back" into an offensive as well as a defensive *rôle*, and demonstrated the fact that this was the right place to put your best and safest man, and not necessarily your heaviest. In the same way, it was found that a heavy man *suitably mounted* made as good if not a better "No. 1" than the light man, for in hustling weight must necessarily tell. "No. 1," then, should be a hard and good rider, with knowledge of pace, and should be up to all the "dodges" which a "back" has necessarily to resort to to elude his vigilant adversary. It is generally, therefore, customary to put "No. 1" the man who is the least sure hitter in the team; and he is directed to turn his attention mainly towards preventing the opposing "back" from hitting the ball, and not to hitting it himself. "No. 2" is the offensive member of the team, and should be a hard, clean, and straight hitter, mounted on fast and handy ponies. The remaining member is "No. 3." This is the least responsible position in the game; in it the new hand may well be placed until he feels his feet, and shows what he is capable of.

CHAPTER IX.

DUTIES OF DIFFERENT MEMBERS OF A TEAM.

The "Back."

The "back" should, as a rule, be mounted on the best ponies in the regiment, for on him depends both offensively and defensively very largely the success of the team. A "back" mounted on slow or unreliable ponies is not merely a weak point in his team, but deprives it of that backbone and stamina which it has a right to look for in him, and which is very essential to enable the rest of the team to play in their places, with confidence both in a losing and a winning game. The general duties of a "back" are both offensive and defensive, according to the state of the game. Offensively his duty is to hit the ball well up into the game; to make long shots at goal; and on occasion, when opportunity offers, and "No. 3" is ready to fall back and take his place, to make runs. Until within the last few years, it was a hard and fast rule that the "back" was *never* to go up or make runs; but experience has proved that a "back" may often do invaluable service to his side by going up, provided always that "No. 3" takes his place and that the "back" gets back to his own place as soon as possible after performing his temporary service. Nothing disorganizes a team more than having a "back" who can never be relied upon to be in his right place at the right time. Defensively the "back" is all in all to his team; a steady determined "back" will often wear out and break the most spirited attacks of a superior team, and may even turn the tide of victory. The "back's" position during the ordinary course of the game should be close enough up to it to enable him to take an active part in the game, in fact sufficiently near to guard against that disjointed play which is noticeable in those teams in which the "back," either doubting his own powers or owing to the inferiority of his mounts, stands afar off and acts entirely on the defensive. When the team is hard pressed and the enemy are within the thirty-yards flags, the "back" will find that his best position is between the goal-posts, where he may meet or turn aside many a well-directed shot at his goal. The most valuable strokes for a "back" to practice are clean and hard driving, straight ahead, and back-handers, both on the near and off side of his pony. In hitting back-handers, it is next to useless to hit the ball back in a half-hearted way straight back in the direction you are coming down, for by doing so, in nine cases out of ten, you will merely send the ball straight into the hands of the enemy's "No. 2," who will, you may be sure, make hay with it immediately. Back-handers must be hard hit and, if possible, in a line diverging slightly to right or left from your own line of retreat. By this means the chances of the ball falling into the enemy's hands will be minimized, and it will escape the risk of being accidentally stopped by one of the ponies that are following you. In meeting a ball which is travelling towards you at any pace, it will be found safest to hold the stick with the head just clear of the ground, and to make your first a dribbling stroke or even almost a "blocking" stroke, to use a cricket phrase; this sets the ball going in the right direction, gives you the right of way, and obliges everyone to clear off from your front, thereby allowing you a more or less free hit. One of the chief aims of a "back" is to free himself from the unwelcome attentions of the hostile "No. 1," by putting him "off-side" as often as possible. Some "backs" are remarkably clever in this respect, and the opposing "No. 1" finds himself doing little or no harm to the enemy, and for half his time is "off-side," and therefore lost to his side. I am afraid it is beyond my powers to describe on paper several very useful little artifices which a "back" may with advantage employ; I can only recommend the reader to play

"No. 1" against a really brilliant and experienced "back" like Dufadar Hira Sing, of the 12th Bengal Cavalry, and he will very soon see how difficult a job it is to keep "on side," and to "stick to" a man of his powers. Finally, our advice to a would-be "back" is, to sit tight, to keep perfectly cool, and not to allow himself to be bothered or flustered by a "flying man." In nine cases out of ten it will be found that the "flying man," if stoutly ignored, will very soon get sick of his job, and the "back" for the rest of the game becomes a free man. This has been particularly noticeable in late tournaments.

"Number 3."

Next we come to "No. 3," working up the team numerically from "back" to "No. 1." The general duties of "No. 3" are to prevent his "back" from being unduly hustled, to hustle on every possible opportunity the enemy's "No. 2"; and lastly, to be always in readiness to drop back and take "back's" place in the event of his "going up," or making a run. He should be proficient in all kinds of strokes, but more especially in hitting back-handers, and should be able to make his strokes with judgment, both as to strength and direction, so as to place the ball in the most favourable position for his own "No. 2" to take it on. "No. 3" should be careful not to crowd too close on to his own "No. 2," for in the event of the latter missing the ball he would, if too close, miss it also, and leave the field open for the enemy. In hustling the enemy's "No. 2," he will do well to hustle with discretion; that is, to hustle only where his hustling will be effective. For instance, it is no good hustling a "No. 2" who is riding nose to tail with one of your own side who is just about to hit a back-hander, for even if the back-hander is missed, the hostile "No. 2" is too close on his opponent to take advantage of the miss. Rather, draw rein and place yourself in such a position as to be ready either to turn and take on the ball hit back to you, or else to cut in and hit the back-hander missed by your friend. In fact, play with your head; a most useful piece of advice to give, no doubt, but one which only first-class players appear to be able to follow.

"*Number* 2."

"No. 2" is *par excellence* the playing man in a team, and his *rôle* is almost entirely offensive. He should be a brilliant, hard, and sure hitter, hitting with equal ease both on the near side and on the off side; and he should be a good judge of strength and direction, and a deadly shot at goal. He must be mounted on very fast and, above all, on very handy ponies. His play should be a nice combination of discretion and dash; discretion in knowing where and when to gallop, and dash in picking up each fleeting opportunity of cutting in and scoring.

When "No. 3" or the "back" are hitting to him either straight drives or back-handers, he should know their strength exactly, and be ready, if facing in the right direction, to pick up the ball and take it on; or if facing to the rear, ready to turn and take it on before any of the enemy can meet it or cut in. Fancy strokes are permissible to "No. 2," but we submit to no other member of the team; this player's stick should be as handy as a racquet bat in his hands, and strokes in any position or direction possible to him. To save wear and tear of horse flesh, it is a good thing to practise strokes off a wooden horse. The rider sits on the horse, and all his servants stand around and bowl balls at him, one after another, from every point of the compass. Dumb-bells and Indian clubs should also be daily used.

"*Number* 1."

"No. 1," or "flying man," lives only to hustle the opposing "back," and to make his existence burdensome to him. From start to finish, he should never relax for a minute his attentions; ever present, ever in the enemy's way, he is a most invaluable man if he will only stick to his business. How difficult and disheartening that business is is only known to those who have experienced the difficulty of trying to collar a good "back." But still if he will only stick to it, the time will assuredly come in a game when his perseverance will be rewarded. A "flying man" cannot expect to thwart a "back" on every occasion on which he tries to do so; but every now and then his efforts will be successful, and successful, too, very possibly at a time most critical for the enemy's goal. To carry out his duties effectively, the "flying man" should have one eye on the ball (*not* with a view to hitting it) and the other on the enemy's "back," and should so time his riding as to intercept himself, his pony, or his stick between the "back" and the ball on every possible occasion. The only occasion on which it is permissible, I submit, for a "flying man" to hit a ball at all is when he has a free shot at goal at close range. It is a very good education for a "No. 1" to play only with a hockey stick, removing thereby the almost irresistible temptation he feels now and again to make runs instead of sticking to his own business.

Having impressed these the broad rudiments of the game upon the different members of an aspiring team, it behoves their captain to put them into the field with a view to trying their strength, and as a preparation for the future. It is advisable to play at least once a week a foreign match, or against a scratch local team, so as to give the regimental team constant practice in playing together, and thereby gaining confidence in themselves and each other. During the game absolute discipline should be enforced, and no member of the team, except the captain, should have a word to say whilst the ball is in play. It is well to inculcate from the very beginning a spirit of calmness and silence in a team. The game is in itself so exciting, especially if two teams are very closely matched, that the impulse of most men is to shout and yell, and make a noise without gaining any commensurate advantage from doing so, but rather, on the contrary, suffering loss of power. A team, too, that is habitually silent and self-contained is not likely to let slip those blossoms of speech which often make a polo ground an unvisitable spot for the ladies of a station. The next thing to be inculcated is the absolute necessity of sticking to one's place in a team, through thick and thin, in defeat or victory. It may not seem to pay at first, and scratch teams playing all anyhow may defeat our young team badly to begin with, but let them only stick to their places steadily and manfully, and play the game on the set lines taught them, and the tide of victory is bound to turn. We have seen this occur over and over again. The scratch team of brilliant players start off by hitting goals as easily as shelling peas; then they slacken off a bit, and the disciplined team begins to make way slowly but surely. From slackness the scratch team go to rot, and then fall completely to pieces, leaving the disciplined team to romp in easy winners. The mounting of the team must be most carefully looked to and regulated, for the ponies constitute three-quarters of the elements which bring success to a team. It is as hopeless to play on very small or slow ponies against a fast, well-mounted team, even though the players themselves may be first class, as to attempt to win the Derby with a troop horse. Every man in a team should be in hard physical training; no one, till he has experienced it, has any idea how bodily training tells in the last ten minutes of a tournament game. Dumb-bells, Indian clubs, and hitting about balls from a wooden horse, all strengthen the muscles of the arm and wrist. Hockey or foot-ball or paper-chases on foot are good for the wind, and a regular hard game of polo should be played at least three days in the week. Too many long cigars, port wine and a plethora of whisky pegs should be discouraged, and "wet nights" tabooed.

CHAPTER X.

CONCLUDING REMARKS.

In conclusion, I hope that this small and imperfect work will suggest to someone of larger experiences and greater literary capacity than myself to write a really standard book on polo; a book fit to take its place in the ranks of the Badminton Library series on English sports and games. It is, I know, contended by some that polo is such an expensive game that it is leading to the ruin of half the subalterns in India; and that inspecting Generals ascribe the inferiority of the chargers ridden by many officers to their inability to afford to buy good horses, all their money having been expended on polo ponies. Of course there is much truth in this, but, on the other hand, as "An Elderly Gentleman" points out, the riding power of a young cavalry officer is vastly improved by this and other costly mounted sports. Whether is it better to have officers who cannot ride mounted on costly horses, or to have officers who can ride mounted on somewhat inferior ones? That is a riddle which each one can answer according to his own taste and fancy. It is no doubt, absolutely necessary for an officer to be properly mounted on parade, and he must, of course, make that his first aim. But why is it considered necessary for a young officer to mount himself on only the most expensive breeds? Now-a-days a respectable Arab costs Rs. 1,000; and anything really good as much as Rs. 1,500 to Rs. 2,000. A Waler, too, if a cut above the stud standard, will cost nearer Rs. 1,500 than anything else. There are, on the contrary, hundreds of country-bred horses, sound, good-looking, and up to any amount of work, from 14-2 hands to 15 hands high, which may be bought for Rs. 300 or Rs. 400; and yet these are debarred to officers in many regiments because they are not big enough, or what not, thereby binding down the young officer to buy, perhaps, an inferior all-round animal, at three times the price of the other, simply on the grounds that the latter is designated a Waler or an Arab. As regards ponies, we have made our own bed and we must lie on it. Not ten years ago, there were hundreds of first-class ponies in the Punjab, which could be bought from Rs. 100 to Rs. 200; and though, of course, the spread of polo is, in some measure, answerable for the enormous rise in the price of ponies which has taken place; yet the evil may be mainly, I think, traced to the somewhat selfish and short-sighted policy inaugurated by a few regiments, who, establishing a reputation for giving very high prices for likely ponies in the rough, thereby made their regiments a centre of attraction to horse-dealers; the result being not only the ridiculous rise in the price of ponies, without any corresponding profit to the breeder, but the incubation and hatching of that curse in all trades, the middle-man, in this case the pony-dealer. We, the polo players, have to pay treble its market value for a pony; the zemindar gets much the same as he used to, and between us we fatten up an army of middle-men. As an instance of this, the following story may be useful and instructive.

Not very long ago, happening one day to notice rather a smart-looking pony in our lines, I asked the sowar * what price be would sell the pony for, and whether he would allow me a trial of him for polo purposes. He replied that he would be satisfied with Rs. 60, and that any trial or examination I liked to make I was welcome to; but, he added, "the pony is, we think, *diwana* (mad), and I doubt if your honour will be able to do anything with him." I spent a month over that pony, and tried patiently all I knew to get him to take to polo. Mad or not mad, he was a hopeless runaway, his mouth was light, his neck slender, and head and neck well put on; there was nothing in his shape to account for his unfortu-

* *Anglice* "trooper."

nate vice, and yet at any moment, whether standing still, or walking, or trotting—it mattered not which—he would be suddenly seized with this frenzy as with a devil, and off he would go in a blind headlong gallop, and no power on earth could stop him till he had run himself to a standstill. Finding him hopeless, I returned him to the sowar. A few days later, noticing his stall vacant, I asked what had become of the pony and learned that he had been sold for Rs. 60 to a dealer. A week or two afterwards, happening to be in Rawul Pindi, I accidentally met a young fellow, a friend of mine stationed there, riding that very pony, for I recognized him immediately by a scar on his neck. Young Midas was full of joy at his purchase, the bargain having been concluded that very morning, and regaled me with an account of the remarkable astuteness which he himself had exhibited in "beating down," as he called it, the dealer from Rs. 400 to Rs. 300. "Rather sluggish, that's all I have against him; been carrying a fat Babu all his life, probably. He 'll soon wake up." As he most certainly did the very next day, when he took young Midas, who by the way was on duty and going round the guards, over and partially through half a dozen compound walls and finally cleared him off like Absalom of old, into the lower branches of a low-lying tree. Midas could make no more of that pony than I could, and sold it for its original value, or rather under, by auction in the bazaar. I never had the heart to tell him how he had been gulled and swindled at the time, so my present tale will be a revelation to him. Of course, what had happened was what very frequently happens when the middleman, the horse-dealer, appears on the scene. The dealer buys the pony for Rs. 60, hogs his mane, docks his tail, brushes him up a bit, gives him a dose of opium if necessary, and proceeds forthwith to sell that pony for Rs. 300; and we, many of us, are weak enough to buy it. Nay, more, we have come across a man who gave Rs. 500 for a pony in the horse-serai at Lahore, being then without any knowledge whatever of its antecedents, or having any trial of it beyond trotting it up and down.

These are, I think, glaring cases of the evil we deplore. Now that prices are up, it is quite impossible to bring them down unless the trade of horse-dealer be so heavily taxed as to die a natural death. Meanwhile the authors of the evil have, in most cases, gone gaily off, leaving us to bear the burden of their short-sighted policy. Under present conditions, no doubt, polo in India is a most expensive game; but, perhaps, many men make it unnecessarily so by injudicious buying and selling. It is a literal fact that untrained ponies are now cheaper at Home, and at Malta, than they are in India. In Ireland, and in many parts of England, a man can with a little trouble and patience, pick up untrained ponies of the right stamp and size from £12 up to £20; ponies which in India would be worth from Rs. 250 to Rs. 400 at the present time. And in Malta we have seen many excellent ponies, whose initial cost was £15 or under. In spite, however, of these drawbacks the game is daily increasing in popularity, and I think most of my readers will agree with me in placing it at the head of English sports and pastimes as the very Prince of Games.

RECENT BOOKS

ON TRAVEL AND ADVENTURE IN THE EAST.

Crown 8vo. 5s.

REMINISCENCES of LIFE and SPORT in SOUTHERN INDIA. By Colonel HEBER DRURY, late Madras Staff Corps, Author of "The Useful Plants of India," &c.

"Colonel Drury's book is not tame. He had some very wild sport indeed, the record of which we have read with zest. Still what we like best in the book is his account of the manners and customs of the people among whom he sojourned."—*Rod and Gun.*

"He describes a tract of country little known. . . . He writes in a straightforward, simple style. . . . Altogether there is more to be gleaned from this modest volume than from more imposing and bulky works."—*Saturday Review.*

"Written in a pleasant, chatty way, and gives the reader a good idea of life in India, the mode of travelling, and the kind of sport to be expected."—*Morning Post.*

Crown 8vo. 6s.

THE KARUN RIVER: an Opening to British Commerce. By W. F. AINSWORTH, Ph.D., F.S.A., F.R.G.S., Author of "A Personal Narrative of the Euphrates Expedition."

"An excellent introduction to that wider and more detailed study of the history and geography of Southern Persia, which the opening of the Karun is likely to stimulate."—*Manchester Guardian.*

"This book has appeared at an opportune moment, when British commerce is being attracted to the Persian Gulf by the navigation concessions obtained by the skilful negotiations of Lord Salisbury, and the writer is probably better qualified than any other person to give the information required by exporters about this very interesting and productive region."—*British Trade Journal.*

Royal 8vo. 21s.

AD ORIENTEM: Travels in India, Ceylon, Straits Settlements, China, Japan, and North America. By A. D. FREDERICKSON, F.R.G.S. With 2 Maps and 25 Coloured Plates.

"His journey in Java is excellently well told. Many of the illustrations are botanical and are executed with much taste."—*Athenæum.*

Crown 8vo. 5s.

EIGHTEEN HUNDRED MILES on a BURMESE TAT, THROUGH BURMAH, SIAM, and the EASTERN SHAN STATES. By an Ordinary British Subaltern—to wit, Lieutenant G. J. YOUNGHUSBAND, Queen's Own Corps of Guides.

"This is an unpretentious, readable, and withal an instructive little book. . An hour with this volume is time well spent."—*Broad Arrow.*

2 vols. Demy 8vo. 32s.

JOURNALS in HYDRABAD, KASHMIR, SIKKIM, and NEPAL. By Sir RICHARD TEMPLE, K.C.S.I., &c. Edited, with Introduction by his Son, Captain R. C. TEMPLE, Bengal Staff Corps. With Chromo-lithographs and Maps.

Crown 8vo. 8s. 6d.

ORIENT and OCCIDENT: a Journey East from Lahore to Liverpool. By Major-General R. C. W. REVELEY MITFORD, Author of "To Caubul with the Cavalry Brigade." With Illustrations from Sketches by the Author.

2 vols. Demy 8vo. 42s.

THE MIDDLE KINGDOM: a Survey of the Geography, Government, Literature, Social Life, Arts, and History of the Chinese Empire and its Inhabitants. By S. WELLS WILLIAMS, LL.D., Professor of the Chinese Language and Literature at Yale College. Revised Edition. With 74 Illustrations and a New Map of the Empire.

Fcap. 8vo. 1s.

A FEW HINTS to TRAVELLERS in INDIA. By AN ANGLO-INDIAN.

W. H. ALLEN AND CO., 13 WATERLOO PLACE. S.W.

Published by

Facsimile Publisher
Ashok Vihar, Delhi-110052 (India)
Website: www.facsimilepublisher.com

Distributed by

Gyan Books Pvt. Ltd.
5, Ansari Road, Daryaganj, New Delhi-110002 (India)
E-mail: books@gyanbooks.com, Website: www.gyanbooks.com

8 888000 686064